HOP STOP
& GO

Fascinating Encounters With People
Around The World

UTPAL K DUTTA

Dedication

"Vasudhaiva Kutumbakam" says an ancient scripture in Sanskrit language – meaning 'The *Whole World is a Family'*. I dedicate this book to my family. To my wife Deepali, to our parents, children and their families, our brothers and sisters, friends and relations; to numerous people in various parts of the world with whom I had interesting encounters. I dedicate it to all who enriched my life and made it a fascinating learning experience.

Acknowledgement

It took more than two years to complete the book with continuous support, encouragement and contribution from many. I specially wish to acknowledge the effort and contribution of –

Deepali, for her encouragement and patient editing countless times, resulting from my urge to improve and change the content again and again; for her contributions towards photographs, sketches, and for recapturing some interesting memories from our travels together.

Rini Dutta, for taking up the responsibility to publish the book; for her contribution towards sketches, reviews and photographs and for continuous encouragement leading to its publication.

Diana Ortiz, Arup Dutta, Mahesh Natarajan and Biswajit Das for editing and giving valuable suggestions on the content.

Varun and Aakash for making sharp observations on the content and clear decisions on the presentation format of the book, with their young unbiased minds.

Last but not the least, Anika for her beautiful sketches including the cover sketch, drawn when she was only nine years of age.

CONTENTS

UTPAL K DUTTA

PREFACE

> *"We have different skins, speak different languages, have different cultures, but share the same home, Earth!" – Ancient Indian Scripture*

It was a pleasant evening at the Wolf Trap National Park near Washington D.C. We had gone to watch a concert of Yanni, the Greek musician and composer. The majestic open air theater made the ideal back drop for my favorite music composer, who uses exotic instruments to create "fusion of ethnic sounds, influenced by his encounters with cultures around the world." At the very start he gave a beautiful statement that defined his music. He described one of the meetings he had with an astronaut. He asked the astronaut what he found unique in looking at the earth from space. The astronaut replied, "What struck me most was that there were no boundaries between the countries."

Human beings are so accustomed to seeing globes and maps defining countries by boundaries! It must be a unique experience to see the world as one. Yanni conveyed that the theme of his music was that *the world is one.*

This reminded me of the overwhelming feeling my wife and I had during the years we spent in Singapore. That was one place outside of India where we lived as residents for a few years. We often used to dine at street-side food stalls. Watching the people, families and friends, dining and chatting leisurely, we felt they were no different from the crowd at similar food corners in our home country, India.

The world is a very interesting place. Two entities that make the world so very interesting are *people* and *nature*. My travelogue is more about people. One of the most enriching things in life is interaction with people. It is a great learning experience that lasts a lifetime.

It becomes even more fascinating when you visit other countries with language and cultural barriers. You often learn by making mistakes – which adds to the fun. Once you break the barriers, you may find that at the core people are very similar everywhere, even though there may be differences in color, size, appearance and culture. Love, happiness, hope and sorrow – all these have no boundaries.

The book is about the world of people. If you love people, I have strong hopes you will enjoy reading this book.

Introduction

> *"A good traveler has no fixed plans; a tourist has a fixed agenda."- Anonymous*

New Delhi, September 19th, 1966 – that was the day I took my first flight overseas from India. I had got a full sustenance stipend for post-graduate program leading to Ph.D. at Loughborough University in England. I booked my flight from Delhi to London. As I bid an emotional good bye to parents and dear ones, I never thought that it was to be the beginning of numerous flights to many countries for the rest of my life.

Over three years in England for the doctoral program was more like 'living' rather than 'traveling'. But I felt enriched with fascinating cross-cultural interactions with the local people of a culture other than my own. More than the sightseeing aspect of travel, I got interested in the cross-cultural interactions.

After completing my Ph.D. dissertation, I returned to

India and joined a major engineering consultancy company in the oil and gas industry. My profession created numerous opportunities of business trips within and outside India. I got married during the early 1970s. Most of my travels at that stage were alone or with my colleagues. Frequent travels continued during the last two decades of the 20th century. In these short business trips, I enjoyed every opportunity to interact with people of different cultures. Sightseeing was on a lower priority.

From the year 2000 onwards, my travel pattern changed. I left my job and set up a firm specialized in consultancy and corporate training jointly with my wife, Deepali. Our children settled down in the USA. From then on my wife and I have been traveling mostly together on business as well as personal trips. Things being totally in our control, we often made it a point to take a break for a few days after completing an assignment overseas, moving around and knowing the country. Our travels have always been 'free and easy' instead of a planned schedule of sightseeing, keeping in tune with the quote in the beginning.

My narrative is about interesting cross-cultural episodes. It does not follow a sequence of calendar. I preferred to link together similar cultural themes, often 'hopping' from here and 'stopping' there under a topical heading rather than following a diary. Start your journey now – *Hop, stop and go!*

1

The Indian Summer in England

> *"Better to see something once than to hear about it a thousand times." – Asian Proverb*

The Icebreaker

My flight to London took off from Delhi airport on a sunny day of September, 1966. An Indian classical instrument, *Sitar,* was playing in the background. I was in a quiet and somber mood. It was my first trip abroad and that too for a long period. It would take me at least three years to complete the doctoral thesis at Loughborough University. Going abroad those days meant almost total isolation from dear ones. Communication was poor, unlike the way we get 'connected' so easily now.

The cheapest method of communication was posting a hand written air mail. But it took a week to reach the destination. Telephone calls were expensive. Direct dialing overseas was not common. You had to book a long distance call with the operator and wait. Telegram was a fast but costly way to communicate. Every word was counted and priced.

Ye olde telegraph machine

After about nine hours of flight, the airhostess announced that the plane was ready to land in London. Now the background music was different. A soft western lounge music alerted me that I was about to enter a different world in an alien land. It was late afternoon and soon darkness would descend. The feeling was a mix of the thrill of adventure and the fear of the unknown, so far away from the close ones.

I didn't know a single soul in England except Manish, who was a colleague in my office in Delhi. I had informed him about my visit. I hoped he would meet me at the Victoria Terminus coach station in London. I boarded a coach and reached there in an hour. It was a cloudy and dark evening, which did not help to elevate my spirit. But the moment I came out of the coach, a cheerful voice greeted me and my immediate reflex was a loud shriek of joy.

Manish was there waiting for me!! To see one known

face in a country where I did not know anyone was a God sent gift! Manish took me to his apartment, which he was sharing with his Indian friends. It was spartan and cold. But the warmth of the Indian friends neutralized that. I located a Post and Telegraph Office nearby and sent a five-word telegram home - REACHED SAFELY ALL WELL LOVE. The next day Manish helped me board a bus to Loughborough. The bus reached Loughborough at 5 p.m. putting me immediately into some of the most pleasant encounters with total strangers.

Loughborough turned out to be a small friendly university town. I hired a cab and told him to take me to a comfortable, low cost accommodation. In five minutes, he stopped in front of a typical blackish red brick house with tiled roof. He rang the bell. An old lady of friendly disposition came out and greeted me. "I am Mrs. Allen. You are welcome to stay here," she said. She showed me into a cozy warm room with attached bath and said, "Sixteen Shillings for a night with breakfast." That made it slightly above one US Dollar. I thanked her and checked in. The room was warm and cozy. Revitalized after a warm shower, I stepped out to face the new world.

There were very few people on the street. Both sides of the street had typical European style brick houses with sloping roof, quite different from the colorful plastered houses in India. I felt hungry. I asked a pedestrian walking ahead of me for directions to a restaurant. He told me to turn back and take the third right turn to reach a Chinese restaurant called Hong Kong. Following the instructions, I took a turn into the third exit which I later realized was a service lane. The moment I took the turn, I heard a voice from behind shouting, "No, not that one. Please take the next turn." It was the same person whom I had asked for direction. He had realized that I was a newcomer and was waiting to see that I take the right path!

That was an ice-breaker introduction to England for me. I had heard that the British were conservative and not so friendly. People form wrong notions about people. Newspapers glorify the negatives. This incident was an eye opener for me. On several travels I made later, I found that generally people are good and friendly everywhere. Negative experiences were rare.

In England, the month of September, one of the sunnier months, is called *Indian summer.* The friendly encounters of my first evening at Loughborough made my *Indian summer* bright.

I woke up refreshed on a sunny morning the next day. Mrs. Allen had laid out a typical English breakfast with cereals, toast, fried eggs, sausage, cheese and tea. Though accustomed to a light breakfast, I relished it.

Loughborough had an excellent bus transit facility. Re-booted to a positive frame of mind, I took a bus to the university and joined as a research scholar.

The Purple Onion Café

My professor had arranged for me to stay at the post-graduate Hall of Residence – Whitworth Hall. I felt more comfortable getting accommodation within the campus. The campus was beautiful, with a lot of classical and modern buildings amidst naturally contoured green lawns.

[Source: Loughborough University Alumni Association]

I started enjoying the culture and the people around. Cottage Pie, Lancashire Hot-Pot (pieces of lamb baked on low heat all day along with carrot, potato slices and onion) and Rhubarb Tart became my favorite dishes. My feeling of loneliness gradually faded away during that Indian summer.

There was a café nearby in the campus, run by students – *'The Purple Onion'*. The name was very apt. Every evening some student volunteers used to fry fresh onions into purple color and make hamburgers with fresh beefcakes from a nearby village. The aroma of the hamburgers was mouth-watering.

At the hall of residence, the dinner was normally served early at 6 p.m. Lots of students thronged at *The Purple Onion* for the hamburgers and coffee 9 p.m. onwards. The environment was always lively with music and a lot of discussions going on at every table on a wide range of topics.

My first cross-cultural lessons were learnt at The Purple Onion. One evening I was sitting alone in one of the tables eating a hamburger. A British student came and sat with me at the same table. He introduced himself as Neil. After some tête-à-tête he said "I am Welsh." I thought he was telling me his surname. I promptly replied, "I am Dutta." He replied immediately, "No! No! What I meant was that I am from Wales!"

To fully get the flavor of another country, one must develop an understanding of the history and culture of the country. Later I found that just as in India the people of different states such as Bengalis or Punjabis have a separate sense of regional identity, even in Britain, a much smaller country, there were regional identities. Mike, a regular at The Purple Onion, never got along well with Tim, another regular. I found it really funny when Mike explained, "The problem is that *Tim is from the other side of River Thames.*"

The funniest cross-cultural episode was that of Harish, an Indian friend, who also lived in Whitworth Hall. Every evening he used to accompany me to eat hamburger at The Purple Onion. He relished those hamburgers. On an occasion of a formal dinner served in the Whitworth Hall, a uniformed waitress came to serve a meat dish. He asked her what kind of meat she was serving. She replied that it was beef. Harish politely told her that he did not eat beef. Surprised, I said, "What do you mean? You had been enjoying the hamburgers at The Purple Onion every evening!" "They are hamburgers," he insisted, "obviously made of ham." I explained that the origin of the name 'Hamburger' is attributable to the city of Hamburg rather than 'ham' and these were made from the choicest beef. He was dumbstruck! Next evening on, I lost a company at The Purple Onion.

Lessons from Mr. Cool

Over a period of time at the university, we formed a nice and closely knit group of friends. We were two Indians, two British, one Iraqi and three Pakistanis giving it a multi-national character. Douglas, a six and a half feet tall guy who eventually became President of the students' union, was our ring leader. We came to be known as Doug's gang. One of the most interesting characters in the group was a Pakistani graduate scholar called Imtiaz. He was a friendly and helpful person with the coolest temperament I have ever come across. A bit too cool and rational, he always had a pleasant and friendly smile on his face.

Being from multiple nationalities, historically not always friendly with each other, we often used to have heated political arguments. But that never came in the way of our friendship. Suhail, one of the Pakistani guys in the group, became a very close friend of mine. One day over some silly personal issues, Suhail and I had a big fight. It became such an issue of ego that we stopped talking to each other. Our friends tried to mediate without any result.

A few days later I was sipping coffee in the university cafeteria. Imtiaz, who had been away on a vacation had just returned. As he entered the cafeteria, he saw me and joined me at the table. We had a brief exchange of pleasantries.

"What has gone wrong between Suhail and you?" he asked abruptly. As I started my side of the story, Imtiaz stopped me midway and asked me to meet Suhail. "You should shake hands with him and even say sorry if that is required to break the impasse," he said. I firmly refused stating that it was Suhail who was responsible for the fight and onus goes to him to try to make up. Imtiaz gave a reply which made a deep impact on me.

"Look here Utpal," he said. "I don't know nor am I bothered to know whose fault it is. I came across you first, so I am telling you to try and make up. I would have told the same thing to Suhail had I seen him first. The crux of the matter is that both of you are nice guys and good friends. That is the important part and the rest of the things like 'whose fault' are trivial."

He added firmly, "I know it requires courage to take initiative to make up after a fight. If you can do that, my respect for you will go up."

I made up with Suhail at the first opportunity. It made life so much happier again. This has been one of the best lessons in my life – *extend your hand of friendship to close ones forgetting your ego.* If it is taken, both win. If it is not taken, which rarely happens, both lose. There is no ego issue in extending your hand, and win-win is a greater possibility.

In the 1960s a large number of Indians had migrated to Britain and settled down in Birmingham. Similarly numerous Pakistani immigrants had settled down in Bradford. London too started getting a lot of both Indian and Pakistani migrants. Sometimes racial tensions used to crop up in those cities. The topic came up during a coffee time chat with two of my English friends. During the discussion I made one intentionally provocative comment just to add some zest to the discussion. "Look here!" I said, "You guys came to India in the garb of traders, fought wars and occupied the country for 200 years. Now our people are in the process of very peaceful occupation of your country in the garb of immigrants."

It was like hitting a beehive with a stick! A torrent of arguments erupted and flew with equally provocative stings, over historical facts. I was being outnumbered two to one. Imtiaz saw it from a distance and came to join the fun. He started countering each of the barbs of our English friends with his usual cool and piercing arguments, getting our English friends more excited. After some time, such incisive logic became too much for our two English friends and they left in a huff. Imtiaz continued sipping coffee, unperturbed and with his normal pleasant expression. But we took it all in fun. Our English friends joined us for beer as usual in the evening, armed with some typical dry humor to add to the morning coffee time debate.

Too much of cold logic can be upsetting for others. I remember Imtiaz's wife, a charming girl, once had an argument with him in front of me. She was very upset over something and was hurling a lot of accusations in a loud and angry voice. It was quite humiliating for him to be hit so badly in front of me. But Imtiaz was replying to every point she made, with cool logic and a calm face. I could see that his coolness was making his wife more furious. Seeing no signs of ceasefire, I walked out on some pretext.

I realized that one need not always win. Sometimes a strategic retreat may be a better option. Imtiaz's calm and rational approach often used to bring in soothing effect to all. But I felt that sometimes one should allow one's heart to override the brain.

Bertrand Russell, was an unrepentant rationalist. He had stated that though man is known to be a rational animal, he could not find any evidence to support it. I presume he also included himself, a proud rationalist, in his search!

Cultural Snapshots from England

Typically British

Living in England, one is bound to get familiar with two British traits. One of them is a typical British brand of humor, which is described as 'dry humor'. The second one is 'understatement' of emotion, even when agitated. 'Dry humor' is told with a dead pan face, camouflaging the intent to make the other person laugh. It is an art of delivering the punch line without facial expression. Plenty of dry humor flows along with gin and tonic in a party. One has to be alert until one gets accustomed to it to catch the nuances.

Our friend Doug was good at it. One of our friends Raman once boasted - "I find it difficult to buy a shirt fitting me - my shoulders are so broad." Immediately Doug named him 'The Broad-shouldered' and that name stuck for a long time. One day Doug and I were at the library. We saw Raman enter through the door. Doug was keenly observing him entering. "Oh! His shoulders just scraped through the door," whispered Doug, with a deadpan expression!

I had a delightful parting gift of a dry humor from a person at the check-in counter of the airport, on my way back to India. It was a foggy afternoon. I was hand carrying a large and heavy tape recorder, the type with large six inch diameter spools, so common those days. This was in addition to a big leather bag I was hand carrying, apart from my check-in baggage. While checking in, his eyes got fixed at the heavy tape recorder I was carrying. The weight definitely far exceeded allowable hand baggage weight. Seeing him staring at the baggage, I told him that I was a student on my way back home after finishing my studies. I was trying to imply that excess baggage charges would be difficult for me to bear. He moved his eyes away from the tape recorder, looked at me and simply said, "The visibility is poor today. I haven't seen it!"

Such dry humors crop up frequently, even in the headlines of serious newspapers. A British politician Michael Foot was appointed head of Nuclear Disarmament Group. The headline in a prominent newspaper was – "Foot Heads Arms Body."

One of the most insulting statements you can make to an Englishman is to tell him - "You have no sense of humor." I recall having read an enjoyable bestselling paperback satire on the strange British ways and manners. I have forgotten the title of the book written by an American author. But I still remember one of the lines from the 'Preface' of the book. It was the second edition of the bestseller. The preface said, "The British have a sense of humor. They have proved it by buying a million copies of this book."

It took me some time to get adjusted to the British habit of expression with understatements. An apparently mild stare or a statement, which is considered by other nationalities as a mild rebuke, can mean severe admonishment. Queen Victoria, when angry about something used to say, "I am not amused." That is an example of royal understatement.

Similarly a statement announcing 'a slight problem' can mean a grave situation.

Some years ago a British Airways flight faced a volcanic ash, causing all four engines to stop. The pilot announced in a calm voice, "Ladies and Gentlemen, this is your captain speaking. There is a slight problem. All four engines have stopped. We are trying our best to start them. I trust you are not in too much of distress." Thankfully the aircraft landed safely.

That was an interesting underplay of emotion, perhaps very apt under the circumstances!

Another common English way of communication that I noticed during my three years in England was *indirect suggestive statements.* I was invited by my professor for a dinner in his house. I entered, took off my coat and hung it. After normal welcome greetings, the first question from the host was "Would you like to wash your hands?" In direct English it would mean, "Would you like to go to the toilet and relieve yourself before we sit down for a drink?"

A famous Indian journalist and author, Mr. Sunanda K. Dutta-Ray, wrote some interesting incidents on 'washing hands'. I recall one of them, which makes an apt conclusion to the topic. An Indian student was invited by his English host in England. After he arrived, his host asked whether he would like to wash his hands. The student replied unabashed that he had already washed hands on the garden hedge outside!

Friendly Encounter at the Dig

In the second year of my stay, I moved from Whitworth Hall to what is called a *dig*. A dig is a single room in a house usually with shared bathroom (attached if one is lucky). It is well-furnished with a corner pantry, an electric stove and a few utensils. This was my first experience living outside the university campus where everything from cleaning to cooking used to be taken care of by the hostel staff.

I got single room accommodation on the upper floor, which had three bedrooms and a shared bathroom. Of the other two rooms, one was occupied by an English guy named Rick. In the third room lived a pretty girl. She was always escorted by a tall, hefty and bearded boyfriend of hers.

One evening as I entered the house I saw her knocking at the door of her neighbor Rick, with a coffee mug in her hand. "I have fallen short of coffee powder and would like to borrow some," she said to me. At that moment Rick opened the door and graciously invited her and me to have coffee together in his room.

She had just taken bath. With streaks of wet hair and a white bath towel wrapped around her hour-glass figure, she looked picture perfect. A friendly chat started and she offered to make coffee for all of us. It looked as if some divine providence had set the stage for an interesting encounter with a beautiful girl.

She prepared four cups of coffee, though we were only three in the room. Before we could find the reason, there was a knock on the door. Rick opened the door. I could see the huge torso of her boyfriend standing at the door. The girl thanked us, picked up two mugs of coffee and walked out.

The girl next door

Both of us were dumbfounded, staring at each other, without uttering a word for a while! We drowned our sorrow with our cups of coffee.

London 1966 - A Ride to Remember

A few months after settling down at the University, I visited London with a few friends. I found the city to be a fascinating place of culture, heritage, art and entertainment. They say, "You can never get bored in London." But something I could never forget was an interesting encounter I had during an underground metro ride (called *tube* in London).

It was an evening rush-hour ride in the tube. The coach was full of office goers returning home. The environment of the coach was quiet with commuters mostly immersed in the evening newspaper. The quietness was broken by the sound of the train rushing through the tube, rustling out the air. It was a forty minute journey to my destination.

I found a seat next to an elderly gentleman, who looked very British by appearance. With a top hat, a dark overcoat and gold rimmed spectacles, he appeared quite sophisticated and well-groomed. I too had a newspaper in my hands, which I started reading in true local style.

After five minutes or so the gentleman next to me folded his newspaper, looked at me and started a conversation.

"Are you from India?" he asked. I replied in the affirmative. "You must have come for higher studies in some university here," he continued.

I found the person interesting and decided to continue the conversation. On getting positive response from me, he followed up with number interesting queries. We moved to discussions on many topics centering mostly on how I adjusted to the life in Britain and some of the funny aspects of the British ways. I got quite absorbed in the discussion with him.

As the train approached my destination, I realized that I did not ask the gentleman anything about him. Before the train stopped I asked him who he was. He gave his name card and told me that he was a Member of the British Parliament. I immediately recognized his name. I had seen his name in the newspaper. He was not only a prominent M.P. but also a potential ministerial candidate from the opposition party. His friendliness, humility and inquisitiveness to know people left me deeply moved.

This unusual encounter broke the myth that the British were reserved by nature. I could never forget the friendly British parliamentarian.

London skyline

London Revisited – 2006

In December, 1969, I completed my doctorate thesis at Loughborough University and flew back to India. During the flight back home, I had a strange kind of mixed feeling. It was a mix of happiness to get back home after a gap of over three years and at the same time a sad feeling for leaving England, which had become my second home. As the flight to Delhi took off from Heathrow airport, little did I realize that my profession in engineering consultancy business at New Delhi would open up the door for numerous visits overseas.

Ever since I got married in 1971, I used to tell my wife, Deepali, the stories and memories of England and Loughborough. There has always been a strong urge to visit those places with her. We visited so many countries together, but strangely my trips to England were alone. In March 2006, we finally got an opportunity to visit London together. It was a business contract to our consultancy firm managed jointly by Deepali and me.

Where Are the Clouds?

I had often talked to her about the cloudy and gloomy weather in London, particularly during March. Ironically we landed there on a sunny morning. To my surprise, all the days that we stayed there were mostly sunny! "Where are the clouds?" she asked every day jokingly. "Your description of London weather was perhaps a bit exaggerated," she added for fun.

Being a dedicated environmentalist, she soon found out that there was a drought in England. She also informed me that people of London were quite aggrieved by the fact that the government was contemplating installing water meters in every house! Water has been so abundant in the rain-soaked England that water meter for households were unheard of. The weather has been erratic in many countries lately. Is it because of global warming?

No visit to London is complete without a visit to a theater. The theater in London, amongst the best in the world, has everything to offer – from blockbuster musical to mystery or comedy. The number of theatre going people at over 20 million a year, far outstrip the entire football Premier League attendances. We booked tickets for *My Fair Lady* at Drury Lane Theater (Theater Royal).

Watching a play in a two hundred year old theater has a nostalgic charm about it. Add to that, the famous play with London of Edwardian era (circa 1900-1910) as a backdrop. It was an evening to remember!

The theater culture of London dates back to the 15th century. London's theaters are rich with character and history. The Theater Royal was first built in the 17th century by King Charles II. The king himself frequently watched plays from the Royal Boxes, which still existed. The building in which we saw the play was re-built in 1812, after a fire.

Two Suave Gentlemen

Our London visit was on a business assignment as Expert Witness in an arbitration case between a Korean infrastructure company and a multinational oil company. The dispute was over construction of a major oil and gas production facility. There were major disagreements between the two sides on whether the job was technically complete or not. Hundreds of millions of dollars were at stake for the Asian company on payments held up by their client. There were legal and technical issues involved. I was engaged by the Korean company as an 'Expert Witness' on technical issues. The venue of the arbitration was The London Court of International Arbitration (LCIA), well-known as one of the world's leading arbitral institutions.

In any such dispute, there are always issues that do not have straight black and white answers on which side is right or wrong. The role of the Expert Witness is to turn the grey areas into white for his client, based on his expertise and experience over such issues. Before appearing in London, I had made three reports on the technical issues under dispute. I was expected to defend my reports and conclusions in the court.

I reached the court at 9 a.m. sharp as required. I was lead to the chamber allotted to the Korean company. It was a big conference room with a long rectangular table in the middle. Along the racks on the four walls, I saw thousands of project related documents neatly arranged. The team of the Korean company was dispersed along the table, looking through the documents and discussing the issues. My client introduced me to their lawyer, James. He was a typical sophisticated British gentleman in a dark suit, a crimson tie and with stiff upper lip kind of British accent. But behind that sophistication he had a pleasant personality. He told me how the whole cross examination of the witness was conducted. My appearance as witness was scheduled a few days later. He advised me to take a look meanwhile at the relevant documents and watch the proceedings. His most important advice was, "Keep calm and cool. Think and then answer, when the lawyer questions you. Don't lose your cool even under pressure." Later I realized how valuable his advice was!

On the scheduled day I appeared in the arbitration room. It had a well laid out arrangement.

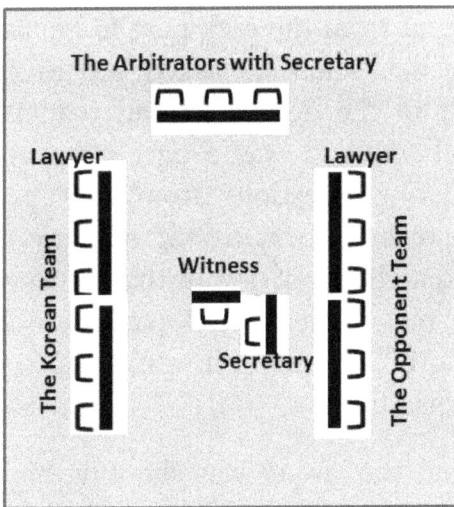

The seating arrangement

The tables and chairs were laid out in an inverted 'U' shape. The two warring sides sat facing each other. The arbitrators and a secretary were placed at the head. In the middle, a chair and a table for the expert witness, a side rack with volumes of reports and a chair for a secretary (to assist the expert) were placed.

Each seat had a laptop in front, all networked together. My turn to sit in the witness chair came. As I sat down there, a simple oath was conducted. Then our lawyer asked me a few introductory questions regarding my name, background and a few details on my work experience. Then the opponent's lawyer took over. He too had a smart and suave personality, like our lawyer. He was firm yet polite, shooting sharp questions on my technical reports with a well cultivated sophistication.

He requested the secretary sitting next to me to pick up a document from the rack next to her and keep it in front of me. Then he asked me to open page number 134 of the document and read the second paragraph. I found it was a part of my report. He started shooting questions from that part of the report. Whatever he was asking and my reply to it were immediately appearing in the networked laptop in front of me. Even when I paused to think and uttered a short "...mmmm", it would also immediately appear in typed form.

I noticed that the lawyer was shooting his questions fast and right after I finished answering the previous question. I realized he did not want to give me time to think about any consequences to my answer to the previous question, on what could be coming next. It was clear that he had studied my technical report thoroughly and he had understood everything. He was clearly leading to the weak points in my report, of which I too was aware. I was replying confidently until he suddenly tore through the weak part of the analysis of my report. He attacked in a firm, polite yet piercing manner, making me fumble for the right answer. Thus pinning me down, he stated he had concluded his questioning.

Immediately our lawyer took over, seeking permission from the arbitrators to ask me a few questions. With permission granted, he started asking me questions on the same point where I fumbled, but from a different angle and perspective. I realized he was slowly leading me to the right answer on the point. He ultimately came back exactly to the question where the opposing lawyer had got me fumbling. This time I could give a firm and confident answer! After the questioning was over, I came out of the witness box and thanked our lawyer. My respect for the lawyers had gone up!

Even today, I relish my encounter with the two really sophisticated, suave and typically British gentlemen.

The Institution Called Pub

After the invigorating experience with the lawyers at LCIA, I returned to the hotel in the evening. I wanted to share the unique experience with Deepali and celebrate the successful end of the assignment. The ideal place to chat and celebrate was a London pub and we headed for one. I sipped a beer and Deepali toasted with a Virgin Mary. Sitting cozily at the pub, I gave her a blow by blow account of my encounters of the day with the lawyers.

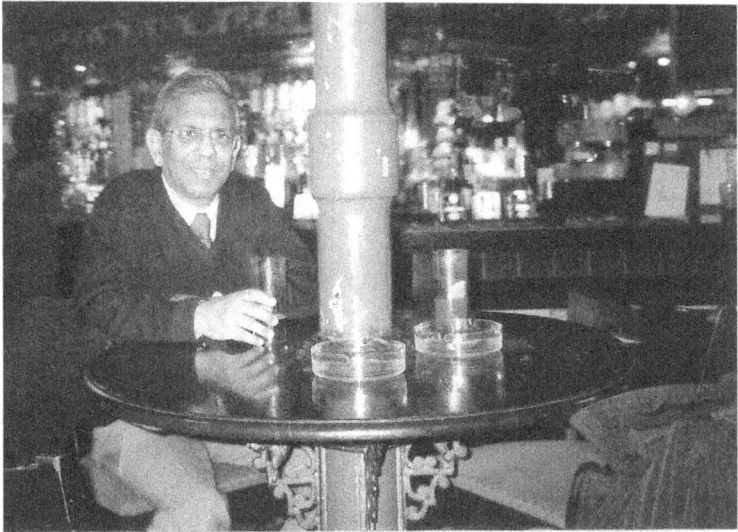

At the pub – 'someone' missing to take the shot

Relaxing in a pub that evening was like *time traveling* to my student days in England. Three or four of us used to meet on the weekends at a pub. As customary, each of us used to take our turn to offer a round of 'Pint' (a large glass of beer) to the others. And after each round, we would rush to the bathroom to empty ourselves for the refill.

The pubs (abbreviated from 'Public House') are an important part of British culture. The pub, in Britain is a unique social institution, not to be confused with 'bars' in other countries. That is one place in Britain, where people open up totally and sit and talk even to a stranger. It acts as a meeting point, as a community center, as a place for business meeting and as a place for intellectual discussions. It is a place for people to come together, meet, relax and make new friends. Each pub has a character, some frequented by students, some by writers, journalists and some by tramps.

We headed back to the hotel around 11.00 p.m. by the 'tube' – the metro transit system. I felt nostalgic, with the familiar sound of the train running over the tracks through the tunnels pumping out the air.

As we came out of the tube, it was London weather at last! It was cold, cloudy and drizzling. Walking from the Green Park metro station to Hotel Crown Plaza through the biting cold and desolate lanes of late night, I was a little apprehensive. London circa 2006 was not the same as London circa 1969. I knew London 1969 to be a very safe place at any time of the day or night. Like any other big city in the world, desolate streets in London 2006 too could be unsafe. We walked pretty fast holding hands, with the icy wind hitting us. In a few minutes we were in the warmth of the hotel lobby.

On way back to the hotel

Our normal practice has been to take a few days off after an assignment. We wandered around London 'free and easy' for a few days. The charm of London got into us. On our flight back home, we chatted about the unforgettable experience of moving around the London streets together, walking along the banks of Thames, the beautiful palaces and statues, the theater, museums and an evening together at the pub.

Post-Script

But alas! Like many good old things in life, the pub culture is also under assault from modernity!

Years after our visit, I read news that the pubs were giving way to glossy commercial buildings!! I was feeling bad about the pubs in London getting demolished. Deepali and I talked about how the British culture and tradition are succumbing to modernism.

Pubs in London are threatened by onslaught of Real Estate Developers, to yield for commercial buildings. "Since the 2008 financial crisis, 7000 pubs have shut down, leaving some small communities confronting the unthinkable - life without a 'local,' as pubs are known" reports New York Times (Feb14, 2014). To protect the pubs, the government was framing legislation so that a pub is designated an "asset of community value." This status provides legal protection from demolition.

Changes are inevitable with the evolution of technology and changes in economics. In the long run, perhaps the countries that are able to get the right mix of traditions and modernism, will flourish as the best places to live.

Good news now is that there is a strong resistance from the people as well as legal protection from the government against demolition of such cultural heritages. "Pubs demolished illegally must be rebuilt 'brick by brick', councils have ordered," reports BBC News Magazine of 24ᵗʰ July 2015. But is it really possible to bring it back to its original look?

A friendly neighborhood

Shall we get the same friendly neighborhood feeling around London next time? Or will it become a show case of glossy buildings all around? Time will tell, but I am optimistic!

"Mobility along the latitudes and longitudes of the world helps brighten one's attitude."

2

America! America!

"Always at home, in ambience or in wilderness."

Airport Escapades

Traveling to USA frequently since the late 1970s and continuing even now, I saw the transition of American airports from very friendly to 'not so friendly'. The change happened after the shocking incident of 9-11. Also a lot of automation has completely taken away the personal touch that the American airports had those days. Where is the smiling and pleasant girl at the counter who accommodated me on the flight under very trying circumstances?

Here are two stories on the contrast between airport experiences in the late seventies and after circa 2001.

Friendly Airport – Circa 1978

My introduction to USA started with several business trips to Tulsa during late 1970s, often with office colleagues. Our American colleague Steve and his family became very good friends in course of time. One thing that strikes a visitor to USA is the helpful and friendly disposition of the people. They greet you easily in a polite and a cheerful voice. But beyond that, inhibitions and social practice keeps them from breaking barriers with people easily.

In one of my business trips to Tulsa in the month of December in the late seventies, the winter was very severe, breaking the record of previous years. It was a longish stay at Sheraton Inn, which was our favorite hotel. I had to catch a flight back to India the next morning. It was a flight from Tulsa to New York by American Airlines followed by NY-Delhi flight by Air India. I went to sleep peacefully, looking forward to returning home the next day.

The flight from Tulsa to NY was at 9.30 a.m. I had booked one of those shared limousines to pick me up from the hotel at 8 a.m. The airport was 15 minutes' drive from the hotel. I got my wake-up call from the reception at 7 a.m. As I opened the window curtain, I saw it was snowing heavily and a thick layer of white snow was there all around. I ordered breakfast and watched the weather channel on the TV. The temperature was -5 ºC (20 ºF) and was dropping continuously. By 8 a.m. the snowfall increased in intensity and temperature dropped further. I came out to the lobby with my suitcase, waiting for my pick-up.

I kept on looking at my watch. Time was ticking away 8.05... 8.10... 8.20, but no sign of my pick-up! A guy at the reception called the agency. He gave me the shocking news that some of the roads were blocked by thick layers of snow and my pick-up vehicle was stuck somewhere, trying to take another route to the hotel. I kept waiting anxiously. At 8.40 I got a call that the vehicle would not be able to come to pick me up. I explained to the receptionist that I had to catch a connecting flight to India from New York and missing the flight would cause immense difficulties for me. He immediately spoke to the manager and told me that he would drop me at the airport by his own car. We hurriedly got into the car. It was still snowing and he had to drive slowly.

At 9.15 we reached the airport, 15 minutes ahead of departure time! I thanked him and hurriedly rushed to the check-in counter. I explained my problem to the friendly girl at the counter who had welcomed me with a smiling pleasant expression. She immediately picked up her phone and spoke to the pilot.

I heard her speaking, "A gentleman from India is waiting here. He was stuck due to snow. He has to catch a connecting flight from New York. Will you take him in?" The pilot spoke something. She immediately gave me a boarding pass and said, "The pilot was about to close the door. But he agreed to wait five more minutes for you. Just take the boarding pass and run to Gate-5 with your suitcase." I rushed with my suitcase and a bag.

As I crossed the aerobridge, I saw the cabin attendants waiting for me at the door of the plane to receive me, as if I was a VIP. A cabin attendant picked up the luggage from my hand and asked me to be seated. I took my seat. The doors closed and the plane immediately taxied for take-off.

No security check – nothing. Those were friendly flying days of the seventies and the US airports were at their friendliest best. They made sure that I would not miss my connecting flight.

Not So Friendly Airports of the 21st Century

Decades later now, things have changed. The shocking incident of 9-11 affected the American way of life. One of the things badly affected is the way people used to travel by air. The smiling, friendly faces I used to see at the check-in counters have given way to either faces looking like FBI agents or dumb self check-in machines. Security has been enhanced all over the world. The security checks in America were minimal and friendly compared to any other country earlier. But now it has gone to the other extreme. One has to completely dismantle oneself of everything including wristwatch, belt and shoes, cell phone, pen, purse, jacket. Then cross through the long queues at the X-ray, and then re-assemble everything. Sometimes you risk a complete body scan. I particularly dislike taking off the belt. Being of slim build, most of my trousers are loose at the waist. As a consequence, throughout the process of security check I have to be on the alert to avoid creating an embarrassing sight.

Even on quality of the airports, things are not the same. During the 1980s, I found the American airports to be among the best in the world. But now very few of them rank in the top ten or twenty. What a change!!

With this kind of strict security, I played a small game once. I had a heavy belt underneath a sleeveless light sweater. I took off my winter jacket but kept the sweater on, with the belt nicely hidden below it.

Thumbs up!

I went through the security unscathed and gave a triumphant look with thumbs up at my son waiting just outside the security gate! No disrespect to TSA, which looks after the security of US airports. It was just a one-time fun.

I have an incidental problem while traveling by plane in the US or anywhere these days. Although Islam is not my religion, decades back I loved saying occasionally 'Allah Hu Akbar' (meaning God is Great) in relaxed mood after achieving some small feats like getting seated in a plane after tedious passages through immigration and security. I used to think saying 'Allah Hu Akbar' was a harmless way of thanking God, who I believe to be all pervasive, irrespective of which language or under which religious reference I say that. It had become a habit with me.

But since 9-11, and subsequent events, I have to be extremely alert in the plane, not to utter 'Allah Hu Akbar' by mistake, so that my co-passengers do not look at me suspiciously or a Federal Air Marshal does not suddenly prop up a gun.

Madness and mean outlook of some people has changed the way we live!

Big, Big and Bigger

First Impressions

During the late seventies and eighties, I made several business trips to the USA, sometimes alone and sometimes with business colleagues. Being a consultant in the oil and gas industry, the visits were mostly to oil industry hubs of Tulsa and Houston. Those days, India was a 'closed economy', where many of the common things that we take for granted today were considered luxuries. America was in a sharp contrast. That created some impressions of plenty and grandeur. Many of those impressions faded as the world became flatter. Material and technological differences diminished between Asian countries and the West. But some other kinds of interesting impressions did not mellow with time.

One such impression is the 'size' or 'magnitude of scale' of things in America. Everything appeared so big. In a drive from airport to a hotel in Houston I sat next to the cab driver, a Texan, who looked big. I looked at his badge which gave information about him. I looked in awe and admiration, his weight was double of mine! He towered at least a foot above me.

The veggies or meat were matching in size - big onions, big tomatoes, huge peaches, big chicken legs, definitely a great achievement of genetic engineering.

Circa 2000 onwards, the visits to the USA became frequent again but under different circumstances. My wife, Deepali and I set up our own consultancy firm in India. Our children moved to the USA from India and settled down there. So the visits continued both due to personal and business reasons, always accompanied by Deepali. The positives and negatives of the big sizes in USA continued to impress both of us.

The Dilemma at Starbucks

I have always been an avid tea drinker. I have frequent need of a healthy dose of tea for inspiration. But I could never find a good tea lounge in the USA, where good quality tea with long leaves is brewed in a tea pot to give the right flavor. So I switched reluctantly to coffee at Starbucks, one of the best coffee joints in the USA. Deepali, who is not enamored by either tea or coffee, gave me company occasionally.

Initially both of us had problems with the big cups at the coffee shops – a bit too much for us to consume. The smallest size of cup for some strange reasons is called 'tall' and it is really tall. No one understood if I ask for a 'small' cup of coffee. Tall was too big for us. In the beginning Deepali and I used to order one cup of coffee each and ended up finishing only half of it. Being a dedicated conservationist, Deepali used to be almost in tears to throw away the rest. The French have the smallest coffee cups in the world. No wonder they shake their head in disbelief at the American way of drinking coffee.

We are wiser now. We order only one cup and share. This is one fun factor of the tall cup - the pleasure of sharing together as a couple from the same cup.

But still the problem persisted whenever I visited a coffee shop alone. The biggest problem was finding a cup of strong aromatic coffee to my liking that I could comfortably consume alone. The smallest cup called 'tall' at Starbucks contained two times the quantity I would normally like to sip. There are numerous other confusing specifications to be told to the person at the counter before my coffee could be made.

Ultimately our son-in-law, who understood the American ways, helped me arrive at the right solution to find the kind of coffee I would like at Starbucks.

The order has to be for – *'Cappuccino, short, extra shot, extra hot and wet'* whatever it may mean. Later I came to know that 'wet' implies without a thick layer of froth which the coffee machine works out. 'Short' cups are not normally displayed in the menu. With these specifications I began to get my coffee the way I like it best. I was accustomed to just three words for a similar recipe at the small roadside coffee joints in India – "Filter coffee, strong". It normally gets me a good strong aromatic coffee, brewed from coffee beans, grown in the mountains in Southern India.

But yes, I have not come across many coffee shops in other countries offering the range of choices in taste and flavor like Starbucks offers. For that matter, very few countries offer such a wide range of choice in quality food and beverage, at a competitive price as America does.

The Dwarfs Amidst the Cacti

The list of big sizes can be endless. But to beat it all are the huge cacti of wide variety at Arizona. Earlier I used to think of cactus as just a desert shrub. But some of the cacti in Arizona are tall as trees. Saguaros are found exclusively in the Sonoran Desert.

These are large, tree-like cacti that develop branches. The branches can be several in number and bend upward. The full grown Saguaro cactus can be anything between ten to twenty meters tall and may live up to two hundred years! It was too tempting to get ourselves photographed alongside the majestic cacti. When Deepali mailed the photograph to friends, someone commented..........

"The dwarfs amidst the cacti"

The Three Sisters

Talking about big sized people, I observed that there has been a change in size and shape of people over the years, since I started my visits to the US in the seventies. Those days most people, both male and female, I used to see were tall, big and well built – with enviable figures. But now, in the twenty first century, many are tending towards obesity, looking big in a wrong way.

But still there are many who are big and beautiful without being obese, as I realized in one of our flights in 2011 from Frankfurt to Washington DC. Three girls were sitting on the other side of the aisle, clearly Americans by look and accent. Two of them were very young and exceptionally beautiful; one could be around sixteen and the second one in the late teens. They were very tall perhaps towering above six feet. They had long shapely legs looking attractive in shorts. Their legs were too long for the space between the rows of seats and were protruding upwards.

Sitting next to them was an equally beautiful lady who looked like their elder sister (my wife sitting next to me guessed so). But I had a closer view and some aging signs on her face told me that she would be in the mid-forties and their mother. She was equally tall, slim and beautiful. The three beautiful women together made a visual treat.

I thought of asking them whether they would mind if I took their photograph. But it was a public place, a crowded plane. Also no one likes to be photographed by a stranger for the fear of being morphed on the internet. But I wish I had spoken to them and found a way to convince them.

The three sisters

Deepali drew a nice sketch of the sight from her memory, as they were walking close to us after landing. If they happen to read this book and they agree, I shall be glad to take a full photograph of them in the same outfit from top to bottom, including their beautiful faces for the next edition of this book. Is it too much of a wishful thinking?

Oklahoma 1978

During one of my net browsing sessions around mid-2012, I was looking into websites on Tulsa, Oklahoma, where I had made several visits. I came across a mail exchange at the website, which brought back interesting memories of Tulsa. The mails read...

"Back in the 80's I attended an outdoor performance of "Oklahoma!" at Discoveryland! It was an outdoor theatre somewhere in Tulsa. Is it still there?"
"Yep, it's still there! See the link below," replied someone.

The moment I clicked the link to Discoveryland mentioned in the mail, a notice appeared...

> **A special message to our 'Discoveryland!' family...**
> **It is with sincere regret that we inform you that Discoveryland! will NOT present its outdoor production of**
> **Rodgers & Hammerstein's OKLAHOMA! for the 2012 Summer Season. We intend to return with our award-winning production of OKLAHOMA! in 2013. Thank you.**

It took me back to the pleasant memories of a visit to *Discoveryland* to watch a well-known play 'OKLAHOMA!' sometime in 1978.

It was an evening out with my colleagues, our friend

Steve and family to Discoveryland, an open air 2000 seat amphitheater. We reached early and enjoyed a nice dinner of succulent steak with baked potatoes before the start of the play.

The play is set in Oklahoma territory in 1906. It is a simple love story of a cowboy, Curly McLain. On a bright and beautiful day, he meets a farm girl Laurey Williams. He and Laurey court each other and pass through the usual trials and tribulations leading to a dramatic but happy ending. The story is told through a lot of dances and country music.

But what makes it a memorable experience is the open air setting in the background of an enchanting countryside, with tall oak trees surrounding the stage. Watching a performance in a moonlit night under the stars created a magical environment. Occasionally we could hear the crickets singing in the forest area around the stage. The audience often sang along with the cast. It was a truly amazing atmosphere. The strawberries with cream, my favorite dessert at the ice-cream counter, added to the charm! I loved it. Later I discovered that there are quite a few such open air theaters in the US with country backdrop. Like theaters in London, this is a must see experience.

At the conclusion of the play, the compère announced that the visitor from the farthest corner of world would be given a prize. Those who thought they could win, were asked to shout out which country they had come from.

There were loud shouts "Brazil, Greece, Mexico, France, South Africa....!" The competition was getting stiffer and stiffer. "India! India!" I shouted, at the top of my voice raising my hand. Once the noise died down, there was an announcement "The gentleman from India! Please come to the stage and collect your prize." I went to the stage amidst thunderous clapping from the houseful crowd and collected it.

The prize was a beautiful sketch of a typical Oklahoma Indian. It still decorates my worktable, reminding me of the beautiful evening at The Discoveryland.

My prized possession from Oklahoma

The Lonely Pedestrian

"Water, water everywhere... nor any drop to drink..." goes a famous poem we read in our English textbook in our schools. Had the poet been born in America as it is now, he would have written "Cars, cars everywhere.. not a soul to see." Those who have not visited America, generally have a visual of the American cities on their minds created by pictures of Manhattan, New York or a crowded downtown of any other big city like San Francisco. But in reality it is very different. Most of Americans live in cities and small towns which have been designed and developed with a unique American concept "Move around in cars only and only by car!" During 1980s, I often made business tours to America alone. After returning to the hotel from office, I used to move around as a lonely pedestrian for an evening walk or to a shopping mall within a few miles, if there was one.

One of the objectives of cars is to reduce travel time. But the well spread out towns designed for extensive use of cars, with residential zones away from shops and commercial zones often defeat the objective. Travel time from home to office could be half an hour at the best, often more than an hour. I have a strong suspicion that the oil lobby and the car lobby had some say in the design of the cities.

Most towns look like a number of prosperous villages joined by beautiful, sleek highways, without a public commuting system worth the name. If you need to buy bread in the morning, there is no shop next door. "Shops are quite near our house – just ten minutes' drive," say our children living in the US. It sounds strange to me, accustomed as I am in India, buying the bread from the vendor standing with his pushcart at the gate of our apartment block in India, or taking a five minutes' walk to the grocery.

Cars, cars ....where are the people?

Most Asians visitors to America miss the community living and socializing they are accustomed to – stop and chat with neighbors during a walk even if you do not know them well, animated discussions in coffee shops and dropping in at neighbor or friend's place with no warning. Particularly in India, socializing is so spontaneous and often intrusive for a foreigner. Most Indians find it awkward to face the deadly silence of

American neighborhood in the beginning but slowly adjust to it. Perhaps the reverse is also true when Americans visit one of the crowded Asian countries. The din and hustle bustle of Asian cities and the crowds may be a bit too much for them.

It is not what kind of life is right and what is wrong. But "Man is a social animal" by nature – I read and heard in my childhood. There is a clash on between the natural propensity of socializing in human beings and the propensity of machines to replace human beings. Perhaps cars, cell phones or laptops have already started converting 'man - the social animal' into 'man - the mechanical animal' in one of the most advanced nations in the world. It has started happening elsewhere too. The homo-sapiens are yielding more and more to it instead of working out a balance between machines and human interaction or a balance between individual 'space' and striking a cord with 'people'. Personally I would always prefer a pleasant person at the airport check-in counter than an array of self-check-in machines receiving me.

But to be fair, Americans give way to man's natural instinct to socialize. During our stay with our son at Arizona, a neighbor dropped in with his family. It was a pleasure to see his children running around and playing with our grandchildren. In a small town in Virginia, where our daughter lives with her family, the sight of neighbors chatting together on the sidewalks of the street was a treat to my eyes. But alas, such sights are not so common!

Football as Played by the Americans

(With no malice towards the great game of American football, and with some 'masala' i.e. spice added)

September, 2013. It was a pleasant evening at our daughter's place in the suburbs of Washington D.C. Our grandchildren said "*Dadu (meaning grandpa)*, let us watch a game of football on TV tonight." Being fond of the game known around the world as *Football*, which is based on the principle of kicking an inflated round ball with foot, I nodded enthusiastically. The eldest one switched on the TV. It was being played at a beautiful stadium with a huge crowd shouting enthusiastically. It reminded me of the football stadium I used to visit in England to watch my favorite team Manchester United.

I was surprised to see the look of the players. They were in nice shiny jerseys – one team in blue and the other in red. But they looked like sturdy musclemen with heavily padded shoulders and helmets on. They looked somewhat like bouncers I had seen in the casinos at Las Vegas. They appeared very much unlike the fast running agile players we see in European football (also called soccer) matches. I thought the padding and the helmet could be due to the well-known American concern for safety and security of the people in general. Though I was still in doubt whether heading a ball to the goal called for a helmet!

The match was about to start. Surprise! Surprise! Instead of the Center Forward passing a ball to another player, an elliptical ball (not a round one) appeared from nowhere, swung by someone. A player in blue caught hold of the ball and started running towards the opponent's side. "Stop him. Stop him! Hand Ball!" I shouted. But before I stopped shouting five or six players in red jumped over him, toppled him and were well set to pulverize him. "Foul, Foul!" I shouted again, already very excited – "Umpire where are you? Show them the yellow card."

The kids looked amazed at my reaction. The elder one was in doubt whether I was joking or serious. The younger ones, looked at me in amazement and said "*Dadu*, this is not Soccer, this is Football." "Football! My foot!" I said, "Where is the foot and where is the ball?"

By this time the game was in full flow. I could see several scenes of almost full scale war with a group of players of one side jumping on a group of players on the other side, trying to snatch the elliptical *non-ball* by hook or by crook. My fervent appeals to the umpire to show yellow card obviously did not reach the umpire.

To keep my understanding of the game, the elder and wiser one pointed out "Look here *Dadu*, that is the goal post." He was trying to explain some rules of the game to me. But the sight of the goal post upside down with the two legs up in a Yoga posture was too much of a shock for me to understand the rules. "My poor goal post, somebody has put you upside down," I murmured, by now thoroughly chastened down. "*Dadu*, this is not Soccer, this is Football," repeated the kids.

Was it a foul??

At this point suddenly I brightened up. Enlightenment and history seemed to have dawned on me. "Now I know. Now I know," I shouted. "What is it *Dadu*?" all three turned towards me and asked with question in their eyes. "Now I know the story (or history) of how the game of American Football was created," I said. "Tell us the story, tell us the story," all the kids looked at me always eager to listen to stories from me. And I created an instant history – all impromptu. My narrative went like this.....

In the olden days when America was under British rule, a lot of English football (also called soccer) teams used to visit America. They used to play the game very well and always thrashed the American teams badly.

One day a visiting English team made mince-meat out of an American team called American Hotshots by beating them 12 goals to nil. The Hotshot players sat grimly in a bar and decided something needed to be done. One of them said, "Hey, the Brits play football as per their own rules and beat us. Let us make our own rules and then let us see who wins." So they decided that they would turn all the rules of the game upside down and make their own football game. The rules that they created were based on three simple principles –

(1) Each and every rule of the British style of football should be turned upside down. Even the goal post should be turned upside down.

(2) Whatever is called 'foul' in the British football will be 'fair' in American football.

(3) Whatever is 'fair' in British football will be called 'foul' in American football.

They also decided that since all fouls will be fair in the game, players should have huge, strong and muscular bodies to be able to bash up the Brits. Since then, the British football teams stopped visiting America. They occasionally came in the garb of *Soccer*, mortally afraid that if they call it *Football*, the Americans may unleash their football team to bash them up.

After confidently putting up this history of American

football, I found the kids looking at me quite impressed at my knowledge of the sport. Even the adults in the house seemed to be impressed. I retired to my room with a sense of satisfaction.

*(**Post script:** Frankly I myself was quite impressed with my own story, which sounded quite authentic. As soon as I went to my room, I opened my laptop and googled "History of American football". Unfortunately the result did not match with my story. But do not tell this to my grandchildren!)*

Cross Cultural Impressions

Things can Change Overnight

Tulsa 1978. It was a 6 months' stay in Tulsa for our team of experts on a project. We decided to rent a few three bed room houses. Our friend Steve said a new block of houses were coming up, where we could get a bargain. He explained that the site was not fully developed yet but in a week it would be nice. We saw the place. Some construction was still going on. No greenery, lawns or plants, all barren – just the houses were ready.

"Do not worry," Steve said, 'it would be green in 3 or 4 days." We rented two apartments and occupied them. Next day when we came back from office we saw the whole area had been nicely contoured with the construction machinery. The next day truckloads of fresh and green natural grass rolls came and were laid on the beautifully contoured landscape. In a few days we saw lots of fairly grown up plants as well as flowers all around. It all looked like an Indian Rope Trick. As an engineer I loved the speed of execution and the planning that goes behind it. That's what keeps America on top of the world.

An After-dinner Stroll

Certain lifestyles which are considered normal in one country can be considered not normal in another. We had one such experience in Tulsa during the summer of 1978 while living in an apartment block with colleagues. On a weekend we decided to cook our meals for our dinner. After a sumptuous Indian meal of chicken and rice, we decided to go out for a post dinner stroll. It was around 8.30 p.m. Six of us were happily chatting and roaming on the streets inside the housing community.

An Indian friend living in Tulsa came to meet us in his car. As he came close to us, he stopped the car and asked us in an alarmed voice to get back to our houses. "Firstly, it is not safe in this area to move around the streets at night", he said, "Secondly, some of your neighbors may get alarmed seeing strangers moving around at night and may call the police."

Most Indians are accustomed to take a stroll after dinner, often in groups of friends and relations. The end of a leisurely stroll at night at Tulsa was an experience in cross-cultural complexity.

I Hear I Forget, I See I Understand, I Do I Realize

That is what a Chinese wise man had said. I had a first-hand experience of it in the USA. I had *heard* that the cost of medical treatment in the US is very high. Whenever we traveled, we carried a medical insurance (available for hospitalization only) and a stock of medicines which we might require.

Once, our daughter-in-law had shown a huge bill for hospitalization for two days. I saw that and *understood* medical treatment in the US was expensive.

But I got a chance to *realize* it much later, during a longish visit of three months to America. During this visit, I fell short of stock of a vital eye drop, which my doctor in India had prescribed to control my eye pressure. I wrote to a friend in India to send it through someone coming from Delhi. He was to arrive in a week's time which was just enough to manage with my existing stock. But disaster struck! He forgot to pack the medicine. There was no option now but to go to a doctor, get a prescription and then buy the medicine. The cost was a shock for me. Doctor's fee $150 (Compared to $6 in India)! Cost of a small 5 ml fill of the eye drop was $74 that too for a generic drug (compared to $4 in India). My visitor's medical insurance covered mainly hospitalization costs.

Yes, when I paid 20 times the cost *I realized* that the cost of treatment in America is really high!

But I must admit that the American eye drop did a miraculous job on another of my ailments. I had severe back pain after carrying some weight during the travel to America. After realizing the magnitude of medical expense in America, I was exceptionally careful about my back, not lifting even a feather! The back pain vanished in no time.

Italian Restaurant at Madison

One great pleasure in America is eating out. The quality of food and hygiene is generally excellent, thanks to the quality control system in the country. The cost of eating out is very competitive, although the cost of the ingredients (raw vegetables, spices or meat) appeared relatively high. It is perhaps due to the magnitude of scale, since eating out is so common in America. The only inconvenience I felt was certain behavioral constraints common to many western countries.

I recall one such incident during a nice dinner we were having with friends in a lively Italian restaurant at Madison. With good Californian wine and delicious food, some lively discussion started. I was talking about an interesting court case in India. A politician's son had shot a girl dead in a restaurant in Delhi. His father who was an influential and notorious politician was trying to muffle the case by influencing and threatening the witnesses (Something like "I shall give you an offer you cannot refuse"). Just to give a comparison I started speaking about one influential Senator in the USA, who took a girl out in his car and the girl's dead body was later found on a beach. Nothing much was heard about it after some initial noise in the newspapers.

But the moment I started talking about it, one of my friends tapped me on my shoulder and cautioned me. I could feel attention drawn towards me from a few tables around. I realized perhaps I was crossing some barriers of conversation. It was either the volume of my voice or the topic of conversation itself. It was more likely the former I thought, America being a liberal democracy. None of these though were considered a barrier in my hometown in India, we Asians being noisy people. I lowered my voice and the things looked normal.

It reminded me the oft repeated cliché – "When in Rome, do as the Romans do."

A Friendly and Sweet Encounter

Flash back to 1978, a small incident is etched in my mind. It happened in a mall at Tulsa, Oklahoma. I was looking for a toy in a shop for our kids. A young girl, who appeared to be still in high school and doing part time job, came to help me out. She asked the age of my children and whether boy or girl child. She took special effort to help me choose toys for them, not normally seen in the stores in a mall.

In between she asked me, "Are you on a business tour?" I replied in affirmative. She said, "My daddy also used to go on business tours frequently and always used to bring toys for me." I loved her sweet remark recalling her father. Some impressions last long. There was something about her, perhaps her simplicity and innocence that left a lingering memory.

A Study in Contrasts

The 21st century created a special relationship for us with the USA. Our daughter and son settled down in the USA with family in the two edges of America – Virginia in the east and Arizona in the west. The short business trips of the earlier days became long personal visits for Deepali and I from India to Virginia and Arizona.

The sharp contrast between the two states is amazing. Virginia is lush green all around. The climate is mild in summer and severe cold in winter. Arizona is mostly desert land. The décor in towns is with cactus and other desert plants placed beautifully along the streets. The summer is very hot with temperatures soaring to 50 °C (122 °F) and winter to spring is relatively moderate. We always plan to be during the moderate weather months in both the places – around May in Arizona and June in Virginia.

One thing common between both the places is the pristine environment, totally pollution free, where you can see all the stars at night. Both Deepali and I love to take long walks in the evening. In both the places, it has always been a pleasure to walk along the beautifully laid out pedestrian walkways, by the side of the roads in the residential suburbs. While walking we admire the flowery décor among the lush green in Virginia and décor of desert flowers and cactus in the dry lands of Arizona.

Virginia - the path we tread amidst lush green

Arizona- amidst desert flowers

One thing we miss during the walks is the presence of human beings around. Occasionally a jogger or someone taking a walk passes by with a friendly mutual greeting.

But there was one exception. That was in 2003 or 2004. While taking a walk along the way in Virginia we saw an elderly American gentleman, fondly cleaning up a very old car parked by the side of his beautiful house. As we passed by with standard greeting to each other, suddenly we were surprised to hear a question in pure Hindi language, *"Namaste! Aaap kaise hain?"* Translated it means "Hello, how are you?" We stopped and responded immediately in Hindi. We started chatting both in English and Hindi. He introduced himself as Max. He was posted by the United Nations at India-Pakistan border during a conflict between the two countries in the 1960s. He had stayed for quite a few years there. He was happy to recount his old memories of India. We too found it interesting to recount the past.

Since then whenever we visit Virginia, we look forward to seeing him. While crossing his house we come across him from time to time and end up in pleasant conversation. It adds to the pleasure of our evening walk.

> *"Use your feet while traveling. It keeps you down to the earth and there are no parking problems."*

3

From Russia with Love

> "Weather is cold, but the hearts are warm."

Russia 1994 - A Scene from Dr. Zhivago

Few would love to travel to Russia in the cold of January. Moreover Russia, under a political and economic transition in the early nineties, was not a recommended place to visit. But there was no choice; it was an important business trip. Our associate from USA was on a marketing mission for engineering opportunity for a petrochemical project. My colleague Sunil and I were to be there as team members.

Both of us were thrilled in spite of the fluid situation there. The prospect of facing the freezing temperatures of Russia in January and the uncertain environment due to unstable socio-political situation did not dilute our enthusiasm.

We landed at Moscow International Airport on a brutally cold afternoon. The whole city was dazzling white with a thick layer of snow. We were received at the airport by our Russian associate Ivan and we were taken straight to his office-cum-guesthouse. We rested for a while before going for an overnight journey by train to Dzerzhinsk, a petrochemical center 450 kilometers away from Moscow. It is located near the historical city of Nizhniy Novgorod, also called Gorky. Four hundred fifty kilometers is a short distance for a vast country like Russia, which spans around ten thousand kilometers from Finland in the west to the Siberian coast near Japan in the east.

When one visits an alien country as vast and exotic as Russia, the greatest comfort is to have someone dependable. We had Ivan, a very pleasant person, to guide us. He told us about the current situation of Russia in transition. The political and economic transition from a communist regime to a free economy was playing havoc with the Russian middle class. It was turning the educated and subsidized middle class suddenly poor. We saw beggars on the streets, unthinkable earlier.

"There are thefts and pick-pocketing in crowded places. Be careful during the train journey," warned Ivan. We were relieved to hear that he would be accompanying us on the train.

We boarded the train at 9.30 p.m. The *provodnik* (attendant) checked our ticket at the door of the sleeper as we boarded. Shortly after departure, he came round, greeted us and charged a small fee for the bedding (a few Roubles). Bedding (two sheets, pillow, neat and clean) was handed over to us in sealed packs. Blankets and mattresses were already stacked on the seat. Ivan brought us a few glasses of Russian tea ('chai') from somewhere with lemon squeezed into it. It was red tea, served in a glass with white metal holder in typical Russian style. The flavor was very refreshing.

The coach had several compartments with four berths in each, two lower berths and two upper berths. There was a door which could be locked from inside. The lower berths were like box beds – one could lift the seats and put the luggage in, safely.

Piercing through the snowy night
[License:Shutterstock.com]

The train started punctually. It roared through the countryside on that shiny moonlit night. We could see dazzling white snow all around – miles and miles of the vast land covered with thick snow. It was like a scene from the film Dr. Zhivago. It would have been apt if the famous tune "Somewhere my love..." had been playing in the background. I was remembering my family far off in the cool comfort of Delhi winter.

Tired due to a long flight, Sunil and I fell asleep very soon. Ivan woke us up around 6.00 a.m. and told us that we were nearing our destination. I opened the window curtains and could see the dazzling spread of snow all around shining with reflected colors of the rising sun. We got down as the train stopped and were taken to a hotel. Soon after completing the morning rituals, I got a call from Ivan – "Breakfast is ready. The General Manager of the Petrochemical Company, our client, is hosting the breakfast."

The Russian Hospitality

We were nine people in our team including our American associates. As we entered the dining hall, I could see a long rectangular dining table. It had eight chairs on each side of the table and one at both heads of the table. There was a lavish spread of breakfast – breads, a lot of other baked stuff of wide variety, eggs in different forms, sausages and other forms of meat, cheese, cereals, and what not. But surprise! Surprise! In front of each seat there was a small bottle of Russian Vodka! Not accustomed to seeing Vodka bottle on a breakfast table, we felt a bit apprehensive.

We all sat down around the table. Eight of us and eight Russians sat facing each other. The team leaders from both sides sat at the head of the table. The breakfast ritual started with a 'toast' by the host with a sip of Vodka and a small speech welcoming us. We all stood up to toast. I had poured a tiny bit of Vodka in my glass, which I sipped as a courtesy to the hosts, still apprehensive about it. But it did not end there. One member from each side alternately 'toasted' to the other side making it numerous rounds of Vodka sips during the breakfast!! But it did not end at this. One of the Russians would jump up suddenly during the breakfast conversation and toast to us. We would have to reciprocate. At the end I found that small sips of neat, pure Russian Vodka go well in the chilly Russian weather.

All of the two days that we stayed, the hosts offered us lavish treats during lunch, dinner as well as breakfast. Dinnertime there was a lavish spread of exotic Russian food including caviar – and of course a small bottle of Vodka in front of each of us. But all that Vodka did not get us drunk, dissipating the heat into the cold climate around. Facing the white snow cover outside became easier. I realized why the Russians have so much affinity for Vodka. I too started loving it as a drink good for very cold winters. Since then I always preserve a bottle of Russian Vodka for the occasional sip, as the winter in Delhi sets in.

With the free flow of Vodka and wine, conversations were always lively, particularly at dinner time, covering culture, sex and politics. One of the gems that I remember came from Igarov, a man with a very powerful personality, who was earlier a prominent politician and a politburo member. We were discussing the current chaos in Russia, with communism gone and liberal democracy not yet in order. Igarov suddenly stood up and thundered in a powerful voice, "We tolerated injustice for too long during the communist regime. God punishes those who commit injustice, and also those who tolerate injustice. We are being punished by God now, for remaining silent over so much injustice in the past. Once the punishment is over, Russia will rise again". Everyone spontaneously raised their glasses and toasted for a bright future of Russia.

I still remember the lavish spreads garnished with friendship and warmth. In spite of the bad economic situation in Russia, the hospitality that we received during those two days remains unmatched. Later I came to know that the Russians love to treat their guests lavishly, irrespective of a local or a foreigner.

The Guide Par Excellence

It was Monday the 24th of January 1994. We had a business meeting from 8.30 in the morning till 1.30 p.m. It was followed by another experience of overwhelming hospitality from our Russian hosts with a two and a half hour lunch session. We were told that we would be taken for an excursion to the city of Gorky. Originally named after the famous author Maxim Gorky, it is now named Nizhniy Novgorod. It means 'the city in the lower plains'.

It was a very cold day, with white dazzling snow around the vast expanse of the small town we were staying in. We were waiting in the lobby of the hotel. A tall, pleasant and lively Russian girl entered and greeted us in English and introduced herself as our guide for an excursion. Ten of us along with her boarded the van.

The guide par excellence

She sat in the front facing us. What followed throughout the trip was one of the liveliest commentaries I have ever heard from a tourist guide. She was a tall, slim, strong and lively girl who appeared to be deeply in love with the city of Gorky. She told us that she was born there, grew up there, studied there and had been living there as professional guide for tourists. She was also in love with her profession – talking to strangers about the city. Every sentence she uttered came out with an exuberance which can come out only when one gets totally involved with what one is doing. Her stories about the old palaces and cathedrals of Gorky made the characters of history come to life. In the art gallery, her eyes caressed each good painting. The natural way the tone of her voice changed with the story of love, happiness or sorrow behind the paintings, kept us enchanted. She made us start appreciating the classical school of painting.

Novgorod (Gorky) had many attractions – three hundred year old Stroganoff Church (belonging to the noble family of Stroganoff) with its beautiful icons and carved artwork; Maxim Gorki's wooden house to name a few. But the star attraction of this excursion was The Guide Par Excellence! Her love for the work she was doing, her simple charm and the rapport she established with us left a lasting impressioon.

> *"The best moment for a traveler is when he stumbles upon something that gets permanently etched in the mind."*

4

Singapore Works

> "A fusion of modern ambience and traditions of multiethnic population."

Landing at a Friendly Airport - 1997

Landing and entering into Singapore Airport has always been one of the most comforting experiences for a frequent traveler like me. One of the top ranked airports in the world, the moment you cross the aerobridge, things start happening with machine-like speed and precision, typical of Singapore.

It was one of my several return trips from Ho Chi Minh City, Vietnam, back to Singapore in 1997. The Vietnam Airlines plane docked at the aerobridge around 5 p.m. As a matter of habit I always called up my office after landing in the afternoon, to brief my colleagues and plan the next day's activities. Out of the aerobridge, I went to the nearby telephone booth (free local call services), to make some important calls to my office. I had to call a few business associates too. I opened my briefcase, took out a black pouch containing some loose business cards, credit cards and some cash. I picked up a few of the name cards and made calls. I quickly closed my brief case and moved towards the immigration area. Within minutes I was out of the immigration counters.

But the moment I crossed the immigration barrier, I realized that I had left behind the pouch at the telephone booth! I was a bit worried. The immigration barrier is the last checkpoint to enter or go out of the country. It is like the international border within the airport. I was worried that I might again have to fill up forms and passport details to cross back into the airport boarding area. I spoke to one of the officers at the immigration counter and explained my problem.

He listened patiently. "Just cross back over the immigration line," he said, "But pass through my counter on your way back, so that I can let you in again without the immigration formalities."

As I was proceeding, he just stopped me and said, "Let me introduce you to another officer so that you can get in, even if am not in the counter for any reason when you return." He introduced me to the officer at the next counter, explained to him the problem and then asked me to rush to locate my pouch.

As I entered back to the transit area, I realized that I did not remember the gate number where the plane docked. The phone booth which I used was very close to that gate. A busy international airport, it has numerous aerobridges for the planes to dock. As I looked around I could immediately locate a customer service counter. I gave my flight number to the girl at the counter. She keyed it in her computer and told me in seconds that my flight had docked at gate C36. I immediately started running towards the gate C36.

As I ran about fifty meters, I heard the thudding sound of someone with heavy boots running behind me. I stopped and turned back. I could see a blue uniformed airport policeman running fast to catch up with me. He was shouting my name, "Dr. Dutta, please stop!" I could see him waving my black pouch in his hand. I stopped immediately.

He handed over the pouch and said, "We spotted the pouch lying at the telephone booth, picked it up and saw your name on it with your I.D. We were going to the customer service counter to call you. We saw you at the counter speaking to the girl with an anxious expression. We guessed you are the person we are looking for. But before we could utter a word, you started running." He then smiled and said, "Sir, you really ran fast. You made me work hard to catch up with you." I thanked him profusely and said "Sorry to have made you run fast."

"No need to mention it, Sir. It is my duty," he said.

I walked in through the immigration again, this time with a smiling face. The officer who let me in saw me, came towards me and asked if I had found everything. I responded in the affirmative and thanked him. The other officer, who I was introduced to, smiled at me and said, "No one can beat us Singaporeans in providing service." I nodded in full agreement.

> *It is said that the designers of the Changi airport went to Mr. Lee Kuan Yew, the visionary first Prime Minister of Singapore, to seek his advice on the design. Mr. Lee is stated to have said, "A passenger coming out after a long journey should not take more than 20 minutes to pass through immigration and baggage area. Design the system around this specification".*

The airport creates the first impression of user friendliness of entire Singapore city infrastructure. During our years of stay in Singapore, my wife and I must have made over thirty landings and equal number of check-ins at the airport. Rarely the system exceeded the stated time of twenty minutes.

The year 1997 had seen the worst economic slump in many parts of the world including Singapore. But even under such adverse conditions, everything in Singapore worked as efficiently. An American resident in Singapore impressed with it wrote an article in a newspaper titled *'Singapore Works'*.

Cultural Snapshots

Singlish

If you ask me which typically Singaporean images are imprinted in my memory, I shall name Singlish, shopping, eating and the greenery, not necessarily in that order.

Singlish means Singaporean English. No visitor can escape hearing Singlish in typical roadside eating places or cabs, where one meets people with not much of education. In commercial offices all executives speak good English. Singapore government, eager to maintain its image as a business friendly English speaking country, strongly discourages the use of Singlish.

It was the first day in my office in Singapore. During tea break, I went down to a roadside eatery to sip a cup of tea with a colleague. My colleague explained that the local tea would be very sweet unless I specifically told them to put less sugar. After ordering the tea I said to the tea vendor, "Please put very little sugar in my tea."

He did not get it and corrected me, "You mean not many many sugar?"

"Yes," I said. This was my first exposure to Singlish.

In the business establishments you hear normal English. But Singlish still prevails with the working class who are in the lower end jobs. When the accent becomes Chinese with a mix of many non-English words, Singlish becomes very difficult to comprehend.

The most frequently used Singlish word is 'Lah' which is used almost with every other sentence one speaks just to emphasize it – "You are late, lah!" with a bit prolonged ' –ah' in 'lah' or "He is ya ya lah!" meaning he is boasting. The accent that comes with it makes it more difficult to understand. I must admit that even after four years in Singapore, both my wife and I often find it challenging to understand Singlish in a hawker center or a roadside café.

The Singapore Cabs

The first impression of Singapore is created as you board the cab at the airport. With several numbered taxi bays at the exit of the airport, you are guided by chaperons, "Please get into the taxi at Bay-6." The drivers are well trained and normally very polite. Most often they start a polite conversation with the passenger, "From where are you, sir/ma'am?" or general discussion about life in Singapore. They are proud about their city and feel happy if you give a few favorable comments about the city.

They are supposed to know all the roads very well. Once a cab overshot the block I was supposed to go to and had to turn back. On reaching the destination he surprised me by saying, "I made a mistake. Please give me sixteen dollars." The meter was showing around eighteen dollars!

The only aberration of such nice behavior of the cabs is displayed every night after 11.30 p.m. The fares are supposed to be substantially higher (50%) after 12 o'clock at night. Suddenly after 11.30 p.m. all cabs vanish. If you see any cab at all, it will have a red sign above wind shield indicating that it is engaged or not available. The moment the clock strikes 00.00 hours suddenly several cabs appear from nowhere - with blue sign above the wind shield indicating *for hire*.

Worship Pragmatic Style

In a street corner near our house at Singapore, there was a small statue of a deity. Adjacent to that, there were a few shops. One day we saw a very interesting sight, which is still embedded in my mind as a permanent snapshot. One of the shopkeepers, a middle aged lady, was in front of a statue worshipping the deity. She was worshipping in typical oriental style, holding a small bell in her right hand and swinging it in front of the statue. But what was she holding in her left hand?? It was a cigarette, well-lit and smoking!! On our way back we saw a plate full of fruits as offerings to The Lord. We enjoyed her pragmatism. After all, fire and flame play an integral role in the worship for Orientals, including Indians. Cigarette after all has a component of fire!

Aftermath of an Office Meeting

It was a late afternoon meeting in our office in Singapore. It went on till 7 p.m. We had a few rounds of tea along with cream sandwich biscuits someone had brought. The biscuits were tasty with a strange and fruity flavor in it. We were so engrossed in the meeting that we did not think too much about an unusually strong, sweetish smell floating around in the room. After the meeting, we locked the office and went home.

Next morning when we entered the office, the whole office was full of intense sweet smell of Durian, the favorite fruit of Singaporeans. The biscuits, we realized, had Durian fruit cream and were left behind on the table after the meeting. We immediately threw the biscuits in a trash bin outside and opened all the windows for ventilation.

Durians on display in a fruit shop

Durian looks somewhat like Jack Fruit. Called the 'King of Fruits', Durians are found everywhere in South East Asia. On average, it is one foot in length and eight inches in diameter. To eat, the outer thorny shell is cut open and the inner soft flesh (with seeds) is scooped out. Durian is well-known for its strong all-pervading smell. Because of its strong smell, it is not allowed to be carried in a public transport system. In Singapore, all the entrances of metro transit system have sign reading, "No Durian Please."

But except in the public transport system, durian is omnipresent. It is present in ice cream, pastries, custards, biscuits, candies, desserts and the numerous fruit stalls. You always get the strong smell whenever you are near anything that has durian in it, or you are sitting next to a person who has just eaten durian.

I never liked the smell, though I heard that once you break your smell barrier and eat, you get addicted to the fruit. I had seriously thought of tasting it to break my smell barrier. But due to the aftermath of the office meeting, I did not dare to try it.

There can be only two reactions after eating durian for the newly initiated - a delectable treat, or revolting. You either love it or hate it!

In Glorification of Street Food

They say the Singaporeans have two hobbies, eating and shopping. Anytime you go out whether it is early morning or late evening, you see people eating! The eating places are omnipresent! These start with low cost roadside eateries to large hawkers centers, more specialized Kopitiums and finally restaurants of all kinds of cuisine and at all levels of cost.

An unforgettable scene in the evenings is the sight of roadside open air eateries full of families, children, friends all eating out, sipping Calamansi (a fresh citrus drink) or beer or some other light drink. The air is full of aroma of local cuisine and sea food, which is a top favorite with Singaporeans.

We were frequent visitors to one such place near our apartment at Singapore while we were staying there. We struck a friendly chord with the owners of a food stall there. After we moved back to India, whenever we visit Singapore we make it a point to go there for a meal. And we always receive a very warm welcome. They still remember our preference in the menu and serve accordingly.

The best of Singapore street food sellers, congregate in covered hawker centers. This no-frills, covered version of street food stalls with sides open can be called a kind of low cost food courts. The variety of food is very wide – covers a range of Asian and partly European cuisine. Huge number of plastic chairs and tables are laid out in the middle with the stalls around it. Though the cost of living in Singapore is said to be high, hawker centers are delightfully cheap. The hawkers centers are crowded, often hot and chaotic. But they are hygienic and cheap, well monitored by trained catering inspectors from the government.

Then there are 'Kopitium' literally meaning coffee shop. These are a cluster of small number of stalls, and more specialized cuisine. The drinks stall is usually run by the owner who sells coffee, tea, soft drinks, a variety of fruit juices and other beverages. The other food stalls are leased by the owner to independent hawkers, who prepare a variety of dishes.

Part of a hawker center in lean period

The eating places are always crowded. You get an impression that Singaporeans not only eat to live but also live to eat. It seems these places serve as meeting place also, especially for elderly people who have time in their hand! Like many places in India, you find them sitting comfortably with one leg folded and chatting over a cup of tea or a glass of beer!

The variety truly reflects the spirit of dining Singaporean style, an experience not to be missed.

The Greening of Singapore

The thing that strikes you first as your taxi enters the city from the airport is the lush green and flowery look all around, starting from the gardens inside the airport building itself. When I used to visit Singapore in the early nineties, it was mentioned as 'The Garden City' in tourist pamphlets. Later they very rightly started calling Singapore, "A City within Gardens."

As you drive out of the airport, rows of majestic Royal Palm trees on both side of the road greet you, standing tall and erect. The uniformity of their height and placement creates a sense of over-perfection. The highway from the airport to downtown is another example of greening with uniformity. The large Rain Trees grown along the road provide plenty of shade with umbrella-shaped crown, branches from both sides meeting each other.

There is a relentless effort in Singapore to go one up on greening the city and maintaining it. Efforts towards it by organizations or individuals are encouraged. Deepali had a first-hand experience of it. Due to her interest in environment, she was recruited by an organization committed to spreading environment awareness. She was given a free hand to conduct eco-workshops on environment awareness in schools, hospitals and other public places. Despite being an outsider, she was appreciated and recognized for her efforts.

It is amazing to see tall concrete structures zooming up through the lush green. Most pedestrian bridges over the roads are colorful with purple colored *bougainvillea* creeping down from the edges. *Bougainvillea* bloom normally in dry climate, but

Singapore is a place where it rains quite frequently. So these are genetically modified to keep flowering despite the wet climate. Even concrete structures of the flyways are green with lush green creepers embracing them. It is one of the most planned greening programs in the world. It gives a cooling effect to the otherwise warm and sultry weather.

Creepers and Bougainvillea on concrete structures

The downtown at night with its high-rise buildings brightly lit looks no different from an American city skyline. The sight of green look of the city gets lost under the glitzy buildings shining at night. Perhaps a bit of oriental touch in the architecture could have made the city look exotic.

Too Perfect a Place

During the tea break of one of my training programs, I asked a European expat who was attending the program, how he felt about living in Singapore. "Everything is too orderly and the city is Dettol clean. That has made the place *too sterile (pun intended) to live,*" he responded with a smile on his face.

I had often heard similar comments from quite a few expats living there, although they always had praise for its perfection, cleanliness and orderliness. Singapore has everything a world class city should have - amusement parks, Safari, bars, lounges, restaurants, cuisine of every kind, resorts and now casinos for those who love night life, all of it world class. Yet some find it a boring place. Why?

When I ask them why they feel that way, the more frequent answer is that everything is too perfect and too orderly to be interesting. Some say it is a small place. Someone commented in a blog, "It feels like an overly regulated and clean dollhouse." From our experience of living in Singapore, I find the statement "overly regulated dollhouse" as a plausible cause.

It is a fact that in Singapore, the rules and discipline are strictly imposed. That kind of discipline and a user-friendly government makes Singapore a very good place to work and do business. The schools are highly competitive, focused mainly on mathematics and science, producing Mathematics Olympiad winners and people with strikingly uniform well-mannered behavior. It is perhaps due to a fairly strict upbringing and mandatory two year stint of national service, including army training.

Chewing gum was always looked down upon by politicians at Singapore as a nuisance that vandals use by sticking it in all sorts of places. In 1987, S$5 billion Mass Rapid Transit System began operations with high expectations. Some vandals had begun sticking chewing gum on the door sensors preventing them from closing and causing disruption of services. The Singapore Government, who prided itself for orderliness, took the opportunity to ban chewing gum.

For artists, writers and the rebellious, or those politically inclined, the space is limited. Singapore has only one major newspaper, low key to express any sharp opinion over any social or political issue. The center pages as well as supplements are reasonably informative but dull. As far as TV is concerned, there are a dozen or so channels that show sports, some local soap, movies and news without opinions. The same applies to movie theaters or plays. The movie theaters show mainly routine Hollywood movies. Unorthodox films are likely to be clipped by censors.

But one can sense a change coming slowly now. During our visit in 2013, for the first time we found cab drivers initiating discussion with us on politics and problems of living in Singapore. The opposition party for the first time in 50 years got some breakthrough wins in the elections, though the ruling party still had an absolute majority. But on the upside, the political leaders of Singapore have been able to convert a poor third world small town with no resources into one of the most developed, safest and most orderly states in the world. During our four year stay, we never felt unsafe at any time anywhere in Singapore. My wife, an environmentalist, used to return from her work in a forest conservation project quite often very late at night. I never felt worried – I knew she would be safe wherever she is.

A friend of mine once met a local Member of Parliament. He was surprised to find him a very well qualified person with doctorate from a top American University. He asked him how he landed in politics rather than joining a multinational company. He replied that the government picked him up to join politics during his high school days based on his performance. He had no regrets. Besides a challenging opportunity, his remuneration was in the top bracket. The emphasis is on meritocracy.

The range and freshness of vegetables and fruits in the supermarkets is amazing. No doubt it is expensive. That is because it is all imported from all around the world. So is the range of international cuisine in its restaurants. Our four years of stay in Singapore has left pleasant memories of friendly people and a very orderly and efficient system. If you are visiting or living there, enjoy the positives. It is good living!

"Too perfect can sometimes be monotonous."

5

The Thai Female Companion

> *"Measure a thousand times but cut only once."*
> *– Turkish Proverb*

A Suit in Four Hours

It was on my way back home from USA by the Pacific route – sometime in the early nineteen eighties. It was a layover paid by the airlines on flight from Tokyo to Delhi. My flight from Tokyo landed at Bangkok airport sometime around 8 a.m. The connecting flight to New Delhi was hours later at around 10 o'clock in the night.

As I came out of the immigration and customs, immediately a group of young guys surrounded me, each carrying a thick album. They were eager to display the contents of the album. The albums were full of photographs of semi-clad and unclad girls in voluptuous postures. "Which one you want? Which one you want? Everything is available – massage,

93

escorts, ..., what do you want?"

I found it grossly irritating, particularly after a tiring overnight flight. Instead of raising my libido it had the opposite effect. I had read that exploiting women for pleasure was a several billion dollar business, surpassing many other businesses in Thailand. But I was not prepared for such a welcome on my first visit to Thailand.

A massage is always a major tourist attraction in Thailand. I used to hear vivid description from friends about how deft and tender fingers of beautiful girls move around the body. They assured me that there are nice and pleasant parlors with no hanky-panky business going on. But that early morning experience at Bangkok airport created an extent of aversion which stopped me from enjoying the pleasure of massage in Thailand, though I had nice massage in other countries.

The airlines arranged an accommodation in 'International Hotel' near the airport. After freshening up, I called the reception to find if they had a courtesy coach to Bangkok downtown. They had the service every two hours. I took one starting at 10.00 a.m. and reached the city center in an hour. The driver told me that to catch my flight I should return by the coach starting at 6.00 p.m.

I moved around browsing in the sprawling shopping complex and markets all around. After a few hours I felt hungry and looked for a restaurant. Suddenly I noticed a few tailoring shops with the display, "Get Your Suit Stitched in 6 Hours for US$ 30 only". I thought it was one of the typical tourist traps. I saw some nicely tailored suits on display from outside. A man of Indian origin, saw me, came out and requested me to just step in and see the kind of fabric he had. I looked at my watch. It was past 1.45 in the afternoon. I had to catch the coach back to the hotel at 6 p.m. i.e. just over four hours left. I thought his claim of making a suit even in six hours was over ambitious. Four hours' time appeared to be an impossible target. I told him I had no time and I had to catch the coach in another four hours. To my surprise, he stated in a very confident and firm voice that he would give me a well fitted suit in less than four hours. I refused to believe him. He insisted and requested me just to select the cloth and pay a token advance of US$ 10 only. He would keep the suit ready before 6 p.m. he said.

I saw the nice range of suiting fabrics he had on display. Even in those days, US$ 10 was not too much of money to take a risk on. I agreed and selected a grey, warmish looking cotton-polyester fabric for my suit. Immediately he took my measurements. He gave a receipt of ten dollars, thanked me and told that I could pick up my suit at 5.30 p.m.

Frankly, I took it that the ten dollar bill was lost. I had a good leisurely lunch and explored the surrounding area. Exactly at 5.30 p.m. I got into the shop with the hope of expediting the guy. I was half expecting that I might have to pick up partly stitched pieces. After all tailoring charges were low in India too. I was contemplating on the consequences and backup plans. The moment I got in, the tailor brought out a packet and told me "It is ready and packed for you. But now that you have some time, you can try it out."

The 4-hour suit

I tried it - it was a perfect fit. I paid him, thanked him and asked him how he did it in such a short time. He told me that the moment he finished taking the measurements, he cut the cloth into pieces along with the linings according to the measurement. Once cut he had an array of tailors with excellent stitching skills, who did not take much time putting the pieces together into shape. The skill of cutting the pieces the right way quickly, is an art the tailors in Bangkok have mastered. No wonder it is one of the top tourist attractions in Bangkok.

The fabric was of very good quality and looks crisp even today! All the stitches are still perfectly intact. It still fits me well. I still wear the suit stitched in the early 1980s even now, circa 2015. You may wonder how I am able to wear the suit after so many years! The credit and thanks go to the God Almighty who has kept the size and shape of my body unaltered over the last thirty years, helped by my wife, Deepali, who is a strong believer in the right kind of food.

Bangkok Revisited - 1990

It was our first family visit overseas with wife, Deepali, and two teenage children, Rini and Arup. We took a morning flight from Singapore and landed at Bangkok. I was spared of the usual experience of being hassled by 'agents' of massage parlours with photographs of scantily dressed girls. Perhaps seeing someone moving with his family, they took pity on me. The only exception was in the hotel after we checked in. We got a nice room with a good view on the 4th floor. While coming down the elevator to have a look around, two shady looking guys standing next to me with a booklet whispered in my ears, "Do you want a massage by a young beautiful girl, sir?" I managed to shrug them off.

The format of family holidaying that we like is called "Free and Easy" in South East Asia. It means not having a fixed time schedule to visit places of tourist interest. Move and see as you like at a leisurely pace and enjoy. We always used to start after an early lunch. Sometimes we took lunch at a roadside eating place near the hotel with Thai Fried Rice, Fish cake and lemon juice. And then hire a Tuk Tuk to move around the city.

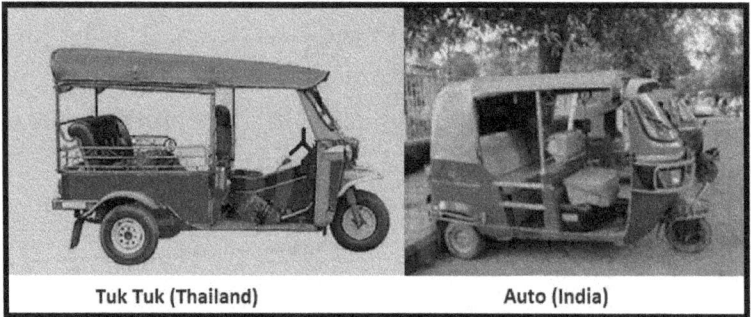

Tuk Tuk (Thailand)   Auto (India)

Traffic jams were endemic those days in Bangkok. One of my friends had advised us not to venture out during the morning and evening rush hours. His office was only a few kilometers away from his home. To avoid traffic jam, he used to start an hour ahead of his office time to reach there in 15 minutes. Half an hour's delay in starting time on any day would take an hour for him to reach the same office. When caught in such a jam, he used to get down from the car and walk to his office, leaving the car to his chauffeur.

We escaped the traffic jams as far as possible by

adjusting our time to avoid rush hours. It was an enthralling experience moving around by Tuk Tuk in the friendly city of ancient heritage, amidst exquisite Buddhist shrines. The only aberration was an encounter with a middle-aged Thai gentleman outside one of the Buddhist shrines. He was a trying to force us to accept him as our tourist guide. His English was terrible – "I shall show you the Emeron Buda," he was insisting (meaning perhaps Emerald Buddha statue). He was almost forcing himself and it was very difficult to dislodge him. After a lot of polite persuasion, I could convince him that we did not need his service.

The variety in clothing and electronic items was astounding – anything from Calvin Klein underwear to Rolex watches and Japanese cameras, from fake ones at low price to real ones at real price. Shopping always was accompanied with hard bargaining. Even for Deepali, who had been quite accustomed to bargaining in India, it was difficult to guess the right price. The seller tells the price of the merchandise 200 Baht, she replies "No, 150 Baht." And the seller hands it over to her immediately with a smile of great satisfaction. After a while she became a harder negotiator with the vendors.

We were interested in some typical Thai artefact. We noticed a deaf and dumb Thai girl selling interesting paintings and engravings. Though handicapped, she was a very cheerful looking girl. Deepali chose a beautiful piece, a multi-colour abstract portrait, showing the face of Buddha. The girl put the digits

300 in her small calculator and displayed it to her. She took it from her and keyed in 150. The girl pondered over for some time. She muttered something and then keyed in the figure 250. The calculator exchanged hands again and Deepali keyed in '175'. At this the girl replied by keying in 225. Perhaps some more bargaining was possible. But we liked the cheerful disposition of the girl and agreed at 225 Baht. The girl packed it nicely and handed the portrait to us. While Deepali was taking out the money from her purse, she wrote 'Thank You' in a piece of paper and gave it to her.

Of course I did not forget my experience of getting a new suit stitched in four hours during my first visit to Bangkok. This time I got two nicely fitting casual safari suits stitched in 24 hours.

The Pianist at a Bangkok Hotel - 2004

It was just a one day-trip for me to conduct a seminar sometime in 2004 in Bangkok. It was the usual official routine of going to work in the morning and returning to the hotel late evening. It was a visit to the city of Bangkok after about fourteen years. It was a tiring trip as it came after a trip to Myanmar and a day's halt at Delhi. I did not move around much in the city but felt that Bangkok had changed a lot. The changes were noticeable. The city had a gorgeous look at night like any typical prosperous oriental city.

But unlike Singapore or Kuala Lumpur, I found it

highly polluted with gasoline fumes. I saw people on the streets wearing facemasks to protect themselves from the pollution. I avoided moving around the street and went to a nearby mall to browse around.

Back at the hotel after work, I went for an early dinner. At the coffee shop a pretty young girl was at the piano playing some soothing lounge music. She was quite professional, with fingers of both her hands moving swiftly generating beautiful, rhythmic melody. I loved it, without realizing that I would soon see a fantastic performance by another pianist.

Tired due to several tours in the previous one month, I was looking forward to sleep early and catch the morning flight to home the next day. I went to bed, switched on the TV and started channel surfing.

The best way I find to fall asleep at night while on tour, is by channel surfing on the TV, normally placed towards the foot of the bed in the hotel room. I don't like to sit in front of the TV for too long. I also do not like to watch a movie on TV. Watching a movie on TV does not give me the same impact like watching it in a theater with a large screen with sound surround by Dolby. So TV to me means surfing the channels, watching news or watching a cricket or tennis match.

There were not many channels to browse in Bangkok those days. I was keeping on turning round the twenty odd channels for a while. Suddenly I got stuck with a few scenes in the middle of a movie channel.

Second World War scene, of a typical desolate war ravaged European town, somewhere in Poland. A cold winter night, a tramp - bearded, youngish man, with torn clothes, looking hungry and trying to open a can of water in a desolate house. He tries to open it hitting on the lid with a makeshift hammer. It slips and falls on the floor making a loud noise. He bends down to pick it up. His face turns ashen as he looks up to find a German army officer in uniform. He is caught, he thinks! An interesting dialogue follows –

Officer: Who are you?
Tramp: (Silence)
Officer: You are a spy.
Tramp: No! No!
Officer: Who are you?
Tramp: I am a pianist. I play piano for the Polish radio.
Officer: Are you hiding?
Tramp: Yes.
Officer: You are a Jew?
Tramp: Yes.
Officer: Where are you hiding?
Tramp: In the attic here.

The German officer gets a doubt whether he is really a harmless pianist or not. He appeared to be having appreciation for music. He asks him to accompany him to his house on the other side of the street. There he leads him to a big piano. He orders him to play the piano. Then I saw one of the most delicately portrayed scenes ever. The tramp sits in front of the piano; looks uncertain. He twitches his hand and fingers which are cold; looks at the piano again. For once you get a feel that perhaps he is not a pianist. Then he starts slowly hitting the piano keys, slowly with his cold fingers. In the beginning it is ordinary, perhaps a bit amateurish. But it picks up and gradually turns into one of the most beautiful renderings in piano.

The whole scene was shot so naturally, so beautifully! I immediately realized that it must have been a great film by some great director. The relationship between the officer and the Jew moves on in a very subtle, humane but dramatic way - one bound by discipline, appreciating but not revealing the admiration. The other bound by fear - but both good human beings. Not too many words - but the silence spoke! The movie came to an end in another 45 minutes, in subtle yet dramatic way. I realized I was watching perhaps the last half of the movie.

I was eager to watch the titles. And it gave me a pleasant surprise –

Title: THE PIANIST
Director.... ROMAN POLANSKI

Roman Polanski was one of my favorite directors!

The pianist at the lobby in the evening seemed to me to be a precursor to the enchanting pianist in the movie. The two pianists, a real one in cheerful environment and one in the movie in a tense environment made my stay memorable during an otherwise mundane visit. Good music is universal and breaks manmade barriers.

The Thai Female Companion - 2005

I was told during my visit in the 1980s that it was a custom for most tourists who come to Thailand for business, to have a Thai girl as a female companion. The girls can be quite suave and sophisticated depending on what you are willing to pay. I had the good fortune of having a Thai companion only once by default two decades later, sometime in 2005.

It was a visit to Hat Yai on my current profession of conducting corporate training around the world. Hat Yai is the third largest town in Thailand. It is located in Songkhla province, in Southern Thailand, bordering Malaysia. "An outpost of the Srivijaya Empire from Sumatra (7th century C.E.), Songkhla served as a port and a coastal trading post where Indian, Persian and Arabian merchants came to exchange their products" says a website on Hat Yai.

My wife, Deepali, a partner in our training company, a petite, livewire person was an active member of our outfit. Fully involved in the development of the programs, she often accompanied me in the training assignments. We settled down at Four Seasons Hotel at Hat Yai, along with my colleagues. The mission was to conduct a training program for an oil and natural gas company. The next day we faced over fifty participants of the program packed in the conference room. A few of their management team were present to inaugurate the training program. On my part, I introduced my team of faculty members including my wife Deepali. But for the first time in my several programs worldwide, looking at the eyes of the audience, I felt that I was not communicating well enough. The Thai participants of the program were not so well conversant with English, unlike other countries where we had been conducting programs. Add to that the difference in the accent. I had a creepy feeling that whatever I said as introduction was not registering with them. I gradually slowed down my delivery and asked them whether they understood me. With some effort after a while I found better response and established a good rapport with the participants.

During lunch break, one official of the management team of our client sat down with us. While eating and chatting, he threw the bombshell of a question, *"Is the lady with you, your Thai female companion?"*

Taken aback for a few seconds, I wondered whether to respond in the affirmative for some fun. Coming from the eastern part of India closer to Thailand, Deepali has streaks of South-east Asian features, complexion and petite look. Often she had been mistaken as a local girl in Vietnam, Malaysia or Singapore.

But then I decided that on such a solemn official occasion, that kind of joke would not go well. I disclosed her identity. The gentleman was apologetic and complemented her by saying that she looked like a beautiful Thai girl.

My 'Thai female companion' did a commendable job in managing one of the hostile members of the client's management team. A knowledgeable person in natural gas processing technology, he had planned to conduct the training of his people himself, without going to an outside agency.

The Thai female companion

Perhaps he did not like that the company management brought us in to conduct the program, instead of he doing it. He certainly acted as if he was not happy about our presence. He was budging into the conference room at every opportunity, interrupting us and explaining things to the participants in Thai language, incomprehensible to us.

After such interventions, my Thai companion thought enough is enough. The next day I saw her joining the gentleman for lunch and having a friendly conversation with him. Wisely, I took a table quite away from them. I did not know what persuasive charm she put on him, but the effect was miraculous. From then onwards, there was no interference and he became very polite and cooperative.

> *I later enquired how she had that magic effect on the Thai gentleman. "It was empathy," Deepali replied. In her diverse career, she had worked as a teacher in a high school. She just expressed her appreciation to him as a teacher, for his zeal to ensure that the trainees got the best out of the program. She also told him that we were aware that there was a communication gap and assured that our team would make sure that the gap is closed. That established an immediate rapport.*

The stay at Hat Yai was a great 'business cum pleasure' experience. The drive from Hat Yai to Songkhla town, the venue of the corporate program had relics of the glorious past spread around. A star attraction was the golden statue of lying Buddha.

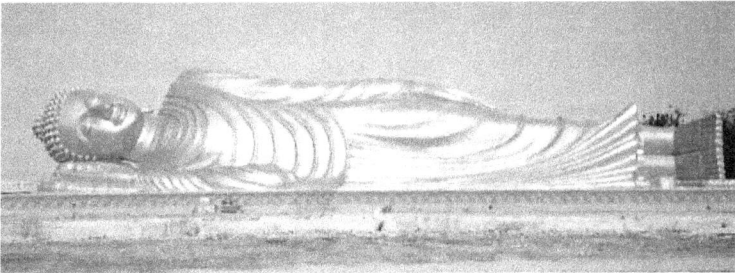

The golden statue of the lying Buddha

Add to that the wide range of Thai cuisine we could taste during the two weeks of stay. The food served during the lunchtime by our host was always delicious. During dinner, we used to choose dishes at the wide variety of restaurants at Hat Yai. A useful feature of many restaurants in Asia is that with each item of the menu card, a description and a colorful picture of the dish are presented. We rarely went wrong in our choice. Generally the dishes turned out to be mouthwatering. My Thai female companion and a colleague of ours whose taste buds too vied for good food of unknown recipe made our dinner tables lively.

While in India, we were familiar with only a few names of Thai cuisine like Tom Yum Soup, Green Curry and Red Curry. There we started savoring the taste of dishes like Phad Thai (Rice noodles with a special sauce, tamarind, lime juice, chicken or prawn) and other exotic dishes made with lemon grass, condiments, garlic and a wide variety of herbs. It is the unique combination of sweet, hot, sour, spicy and salty that gives Thai food a special taste.

Of the wide range of cuisines we had tasted in different parts of the world, we loved the Thai fare the best. It was a memorable trip with my *Thai Female Companion*!

"At the table with family and good friends you tend to become younger." – Italian Proverb

---

6

Glimpses of the World

> *"Paris enchants and then slowly seduces you."*

A Glimpse of Paris

The Gypsy Girl in Paris Metro

It was a weekend of September 1981. My colleagues Muthu, Ramesh, Vir and I were on our way back from a business trip to Pau, a small city in Southern France. We reached Paris by the morning flight from Pau to catch our flight back to Delhi. The flight was in the late evening. We dumped our luggage in the left luggage enclosure and took a ride to the city for sightseeing. The city looked amazingly beautiful. The serene environment created by the classic structures, objects of art all around and the elegantly dressed people along the streets sets Paris apart from other cities. We were using the dependable Paris metro rail to move from one place to another.

Everything was moving according to our plan. But suddenly a dramatic event happened during a metro ride. The metro was quite crowded with weekend tourists. The four of us were sitting close to the door. In one of the metro stations a group of gypsies, around eight in number, at least four of them girls, boarded the trains. Their colorful dresses and appearance immediately caught our attention. They were all standing together in the passage in front of the door, close to our seat. The girls had a rustic beauty about them not found in a normal city girl. One of the girls was particularly beautiful. As we looked at her she stared back. For some reason she was looking more often towards Muthu with an occasional smile on her lips.

An enigmatic gypsy girl

The train started slowing down near one of the stations. Suddenly the girl asked Muthu to get up, embraced him firmly with one of her hands around his waist and planted a long and deep passionate kiss on his lips. We were stunned! We Indians are not accustomed to being kissed like that in public, more so by a stranger. Muthu was almost paralyzed in awe. The train stopped. The whole group of gypsies disembarked quickly. The girl threw a kiss with her hands to Muthu while getting down.

Muthu regained his senses only after the train started. Suddenly he jumped up and shouted some incomprehensible words. His jacket side pocket where he had kept his wallet with all the cash and cards was empty!!

Paris, Je t'aime

More than two decades later, circa 2005, Deepali and I could plan a trip to Paris. This time our trip was purely as visitors in our style of 'free and easy'.

Some well-known directors made a film on Paris titled 'Paris, je t'aime' meaning 'Paris, I Love You', with 20 stories on the common theme of love. The most often quoted impressions of Paris are 'the most beautiful city on the earth', 'the most romantic city in the world', 'a city of love and romance' and many other epithets for love and beauty. It is difficult to form an impression of the culture and people in such short visits to a city which gets such tributes. I can only talk about my first impressions.

Our interaction with people was limited to mostly stopping someone to ask directions to reach some place. We needed help also for ordering the food at restaurants or buying tickets in museums. Language was a barrier sometimes. For help from a fellow pedestrian, "Parlez vous Anglais?" was the first question we asked. Often we got a negative response or a brief "Un petit peu," meaning a little bit. The younger generation seemed to be more familiar with English. But whoever knew even a little bit of English was always helpful, painstakingly trying to give us directions.

Paris is known as the fashion capital of the world. I do not know much about fashion. One thing very noticeable is that Parisians generally dress quite elegantly, move around with a gait and style not normally seen in other places. Even shoes the girls wear look more stylish. Parisians, both male and female generally seem to have a good figure – neither overweight nor lean, neither too tall nor too short. There were of course extremes, but the look of an average Parisian is elegant.

But what gives Paris an altogether different look is the numerous buildings with beautiful architecture. Unlike many European towns, they are often light in color enhancing the brightness of the city. Add to it the exquisite sculptures all around, the river Seine, picturesque bridges beautifully adorned, roadside artists, musicians playing romantic melodies and couples walking holding hands. The presence of freelance artists in numerous tourist spots in the city is a fascinating sight. Besides drawing portraits of tourists, they display numerous creations of their own. One such artist caught us. He very quickly cut out our profiles with deft fingers, from a black paper. In no time, he gave a nice finish by pasting the silhouettes over white cards and handed it over to us, almost like a magic!

On the downside, one has to be very careful in the tourist places and entertainment spots. After being short-changed in a few places, we were treading our path carefully. Even in a foreign exchange counter at Montmartre, we got short-changed for not having read some fine prints carefully, on the service charges displayed on the board. Barring that, it was really one of the most fulfilling experiences leaving behind some lasting memories.

Deepali and I took a view of the city from the top of Montmartre, standing at the ramparts of Basilica de Sacré-Cœur, the big white church. We vividly remember the feeling of ecstasy as we stood there holding our hands. The panoramic view of the neighborhood in a misty afternoon looked really beautiful and romantic. No wonder the surrounding neighborhood had nurtured some of the greatest classical artists and writers.

I could not check the temptation of putting here a beautiful sketch of the Eiffel Tower drawn by an unknown artist. Or is he well known? I could not read the name of the artist in his signature. But I express my gratitude to him for depicting the mystic and romantic fervor of a Paris evening so beautifully.

The Eiffel Tower, a picture of beauty and serenity

In the Land of Zero Defect

A Perfect Business Deal

My first encounter with the Japanese people was in a business meeting at my office in India in 1979. It was a meeting to finalize an order for a large natural gas compressor with a Japanese company. A team from Japan came for discussion. They and our team sat in the conference room face to face.

We observed two interesting things. While in our Indian team each member was speaking on issues related to his own specialization, in the Japanese team only their team leader did all the talking. The rest sat with bowed heads in stoic silence listening to the deliberations. Only when in doubt on some point, the leader would turn towards a colleague, exchange opinions in Japanese, and then he would speak to us.

The Japanese have very well structured business customs. As an example, while exchanging business cards one has to give due respect to each other. When receiving a business card, the card is to be held with both the hands at the top two corners. Read the card carefully (or at least pretend to). Place the card carefully on the table during discussion and place it in your card case or at least in your front pocket while leaving. To shove someone's business card into a back pocket or wallet in front of them can be offending.

The second interesting observation was that on every point when our team spoke, their team leader nodded his head in a manner as if he was in agreement with us. But after a while he would talk to his colleagues in Japanese and sometimes he would come out with a negative response. During the tea break I politely asked him what nodding the head implied in Japanese custom. He understood the cultural gap and explained, "When I nod with my head it means your point is understood and I shall get back to you. Whether I agree or disagree I tell you after discussion with my colleagues." Saying a straight blunt "No" during a meeting is "No, No" for a Japanese.

Eventually we placed the order for the equipment with them. One of the terms of the order was that they would get their detailed manufacturing specifications reviewed by us, at their office in Tokyo within three months. We got a call for a review meeting at Tokyo well within three months from the stipulated date.

On a cold morning of 1979 three of us landed at Tokyo's Narita Airport. After completing the immigration formalities and customs, we came out to the arrival hall. Surprise! Surprise! Two Japanese gentlemen came forward and greeted us. They presented us with their name cards. They were from the same company we had come to visit. Although we never asked anyone from their side to receive us at the airport, they had found out from our office about our bookings and were there to receive us. They had arranged a car for us. We could not help but notice the large, sparklingly clean black Nissan and the milky white spotless seat cover!

The next day, we had a meeting with our equipment supplier. They took the three of us to the conference room. We exchanged our visiting cards in Japanese style and were served with green Japanese tea.

We found six sets of specification documents and drawings kept for us on the table. When we asked why six sets, they opened our order copy and showed us a line reading, 'Six sets of document should be presented for the review of the specifications'. We had put this on the contract without much thought on how many people from our team would be there for review. But they were precise to the word!

Back in India, we saw the ultimate in Japanese perfection when their machine was installed in our plant. The natural gas compressor driven by a gas turbine was only one of hundreds of equipment piped together in the big natural gas plant. Our team was busy late at night testing and checking various systems. The compressor supplied by the Japanese was already fully tested and was to be handed over to us the next day.

During the late hours of night we found two of the Japanese engineers doing something with thin paint brushes, normally used by the artists. We asked them what they were busy with. They said there were a few scratches on the body of the equipment which they were touching up. We noticed that the whole equipment was beautifully finished and the scratches were barely noticeable. We told them there was no need and they could return to their hotel. But their reply amazed us. "This is our baby till tonight. Tomorrow we have to hand it over to you officially. We want to give it to you in absolutely perfect shape," they said, and continued with the work.

Tokyo, the First Impressions

The first impressions of Tokyo were spell-binding. It is the world's biggest and most populated city, also perhaps with the highest in population density. But everything appeared to be very orderly. As an engineer, the most mind-boggling thing I noted was the construction of the city at multiple levels.

Massive highway cross section at a city center

[License: Shutterstock.com]

The underground multilevel metro system, tall buildings with five or six levels going down below the ground and multiple levels of roads and monorail on the surface, dispersed the crowd in a seamless manner. The downtown was just as congested with buildings as London or New York. It is a wonder how they built so many levels of transportation below and above the ground in such a congested space.

Extensive use of electronics in every aspect of life even at that time (1979) was amazing. Even in the land of Sony and JVC, we did not expect so much of electronics everywhere. Sitting in a small roadside café for snacks and coffee, we found that even the table top, made of glass, had electronic game panels under it and buttons on top of the table. Order your coffee and keep playing till your coffee is served! Even in America, we did not see so much of electronics.

A Perfect Departure

It was a day before our departure. I was informed that the next morning a coach would pick me up at 9.00 a.m. I told the reception about it and left instructions to wake me up at 7.00 a.m.

I was woken up at 7.00 a.m. as per instructions I had left. I had a good breakfast and completed my packing. At 8.35 a.m. I got a call from the reception that a bellboy would come to pick up my baggage. In a few minutes, I was at the lobby, waiting along with fellow passengers for the coach. The coach arrived at 8.40 a.m. The driver got down, went to the snack bar in the lobby and ordered a green tea. I was wondering whether he had enough time to enjoy the drink. But it all happened on time with machinelike precision.

Just ten minutes before nine i.e. 8.50 a.m. he came, requested us to board and quickly placed the luggage in the boot below the bus. He got into the driver's seat at 8.55 a.m. He waited looking at the clock above the windshield. Exactly at 08.59.50 hours he started the engine. Exactly at 09.00.00 hours the coach started moving.

The unusual cultural trait, not found in other parts of the world, can cause tension. In the Japanese culture, failure is not an option. A failed mission sometimes drives the Japanese to *Hara-Kiri, (a ritual suicide, as an honorable alternative to disgrace)*. I recall long back I read a piece of news about food poisoning in a major airline. The news reporter reporting this incident noted, "This happens sometimes. But in a Japanese Airlines under similar situation once, the steward committed *Hara-Kiri*".

Once while enjoying the famous *Kobe Steak*, with a Japanese business colleague in Tokyo, I happily commented that I liked the life and culture in Japan. "How long have you been here?" he quipped. "Four days," I replied. "Stay here four months and lead our type of life. You may change your opinion," he said.

Yes, on a short visit one cannot really get an idea of the life in a country. What I saw was the culture of perfection and politeness in the land of zero defect. There are many facets of life.

Yangon – 2004

In the Time-warp

It was late night at the Delhi airport. Even for a seasoned traveler like me, waiting to board a Myanmar Airlines flight to Yangon (Rangoon) was full of anticipation. The flight to Bangkok via Yangon was on time. I boarded with my business colleague Ramesh. It was a small plane. The narrow interior of the plane with only three passengers in a row (two on one side and one on the other side of aisle) was a new experience for me in international flying.

The crew was polite and courteous. They made us as comfortable as possible within the limited space, with about 40 passengers on board. After about three hours of flight the plane landed at Yangon. Only two passengers de-planed, Ramesh and me. The airport building was a beautiful old building with temple architecture. It appeared totally empty. As we approached the immigration counter, two immigration officials appeared out of nowhere and checked our papers. They let us in without questioning.

I got the first feel of the city as we drove towards the hotel. It was early hours of the morning. We drove through the near-empty streets of Yangon, amidst lush green trees, old blocks of houses, chirping birds and occasional sight of *pagodas (Buddhist shrines)*. The air smelled wet and fresh. The only expressions that came to my mind were 'serene' and 'exotic'!

Our host had arranged the hotel and checking-in was smooth. The receptionist asked for a deposit for phone calls and miscellaneous expenses which were not to be paid by the host. I pulled out my credit card and got my first shock. I was told that international credit cards were not accepted in Myanmar! A frequent traveler, I normally feel quite comfortable to travel with only a few hundred Dollars and credit cards in my pocket. For the first time, I felt my comfort level going down! The cash in my wallet was too little to survive for the few days in Myanmar. My colleague Ramesh, came to my rescue.

My second shock was when I got into my room and turned on my cell phone. I could not get connected. To my dismay, I learnt that international roaming was not available! I realized I was no longer connected to the rest of the world! After several hours I got the opportunity to book a call home through the operator!

For the next few days in Myanmar, I realized how international sanctions and closed-door policies of the military junta had cut off communications with the rest of the world and put the country on a time warp. Our business representative at Yangon picked us up from the hotel for the day's meetings. She was a young lady with immense self-confidence. "I am Syu. Welcome to Myanmar," she said. Syu was in advanced stage of pregnancy and yet very active with complete control of things. Her husband, who was present in all the meetings, attired in traditional costume of "longyi" (sarong) and "eingyi" (shirt) with gold buttons and wearing gold rimmed spectacles, was mostly silent. He appeared to be her silent partner in the business, in more of a decorative role. Or perhaps he had some role to play! She did all the talking. Her understanding of the business scenario in Myanmar was excellent. I came to know later that in Myanmar, often it is the woman who controls the show with the husband playing a very minor role in the business.

We drove through crowded streets. The old buildings had typical oriental type eye-catching architecture. The layout of the city appeared familiar to me, resembling major Indian cities. The people around looked very friendly and polite. I could see some beautiful modern office blocks too. Syu told us that these buildings were built with the hope of economy growing at the same pace as Thailand or Malaysia as a part of the ASEAN group. But international sanctions had left the infrastructure underutilized. The cars on the road were old Toyota models running on low grade gasoline, emitting fumes and smell of un-burnt hydrocarbons.

The biggest surprise came when I made my visit to an old petroleum refinery near Yangon. My task was to find out what kind of upgrading or modification it needed and identify the business prospects. The refinery I saw in Myanmar in 2004, reminded me of my first job in a refinery in India, 40 years ago in 1964, in terms of technology of the whole process system. The equipment were vintage. The control room instruments were ancient with huge mechanically run pens and charts for recording. A beautiful country, an ancient civilization of nice and friendly people, caught in the time warp!

Ramesh who was quite familiar with Myanmar, took me for sight-seeing in the evening. Our first stop was at the Shwedagon Pagoda, the most ancient Pagoda in Myanmar, built 2000 years ago. It is a huge golden pagoda on top of a hill with numerous statues of Buddha in calm and serene postures around it.

The pagoda with its gold plated surface dazzling in the moon-lit night, looked majestic and beautiful. Perhaps one of the best sights in the world!

The Shwedagon Pagoda, shining in moonlight

It was humbling and calming to the mind. Sitting at

the feet of Buddha quietly, I could visualize how Buddhism spread around Asia without a fight or a holy war. Its sheer message of love, peace, harmony and tranquility won over millions without a fight.

The Tomb of the Last Emperor

Ramesh told me that no visit to Myanmar by an Indian can be complete without a visit to the tomb of Bahadur Shah Zafar, the last Mughal Emperor of India. To understand the significance, let us go back to the 18th century India when India and Myanmar (called Burma) both were part of the British empire.

The Mughals ruled India effectively from the 16th to 18th century. The Mughals came as invaders from Turkey, but unlike the British they assimilated themselves with India and made India their homeland. Around early 19th century, the British had made inroads and captured vast parts of India. The British ruled till 1947 but remained aliens. The year 1857 saw the first major rebellion against the British. The rebel Indians persuaded the then ailing Mughal Emperor Bahadur Shah Zafar, to be their leader.

The rebellion was crushed. Bahadur Shah was banished by the British to Rangoon, for his role in the mutiny, of which he had become a leader and an icon. On the 6th November 1862, Bahadur Shah Zafar, the last Indian emperor, died at the age of 87, ailing and bedridden in an alien land – Burma (Myanmar).

The last emperor had only one desire before his death,

to be buried in Delhi, for which he made earnest appeals to the British Government. A poet and a religious person, he was respected for his secular views. He had kept a graveyard ready for himself, near a shrine in South of New Delhi. The location he chose was close to the existing *Qutab Minar,* the tallest brick minaret in the world built in the 14th century. But the British did not want 'the symbol of mutiny' to be buried in India. They wanted his grave to be lost and forgotten!

Bahadur Shah Zafar was buried in secrecy by the British near his small abode in Yangon. His grave was a simple brick pit covered with soil, so that the place itself would be forgotten. It was rediscovered by chance when some construction started there. Today it is a site of pilgrimage for many Indians, as Bahadur Shah Zafar has gained a posthumous reputation as a saint. An outstanding poet, he composed his own epitaph –

> *Lagta nahin hai jee mera ujre bayar mein.........*
> *(My heart is not happy, in this alien land...)*
>
> *Kitnaa hai bad-naseeb "Zafar" dafn ke liye,*
> *Do Ghaz zameen bhi na mili kuu-e-yaar mein.*
> *(How unlucky Zafar is! For burial,*
> *even two yards of land were not to be had in the*
> *land of the beloved.)*

Bahadur Shah Zafar wrote: "Who would come to my grave to pray? Or bring me a bunch of flowers? Who would light a candle for me? I am nothing but a gloomy tomb." Mr. A.P.J Kalam, the 11th President of independent India, visited the tomb, sometime during his tenure (2002-2007). He wrote in the visitors' book "You wrote who will come to my grave. Today on behalf of my nation I have come, prayed and lit candles. May your soul rest in peace!"

Standing there at the desolate tomb, I felt from my heart the anguish of the last Indian Emperor, who was not allowed his last wish for a burial in India. You can really feel the pain and sorrow of the last Mughal Emperor. The pain of living far away from his beloved land and people, waiting for his death in a small house in the wilderness of an alien country.

With Due Respect to Our Ancestors!

On November 16, 2014, the President of India planned a visit to the holy city of Vrindavan. The city located in the state of *Uttar Pradesh* in India is known as the birth place of legendary Lord Krishna. It is said that Lord Krishna's sermons created *'Bhagavad Gita'*, revered Hindu scripture defining the philosophy of life.

> *The Bhagavad Gita, often referred as the Gita, is a 700-verse Hindu scripture in Sanskrit. It is believed that the Gita came into existence in the third or fourth millennium BCE.*

The President normally wears spectacles. But he was advised that during the visit he should wear contact lenses instead. Why? Why? To understand why, let me first tell about a few incidents.

Let us turn the clock back to Circa 2004. Deepali and I were holidaying in the pristine environment of Mussoorie, a hill town at an elevation of 1880 meters (6200 feet) in the Himalayas. The sights of some of the highest snow clad mountain ranges far away during the day and lush green forests around created a magical charm. At night, the glittering town of Dehradun way down in the valley below was spell binding.

One afternoon we decided to trek to Lal Tibba, the highest point near Mussoorie. It was a 420 meters (1400 feet) climb over a distance of eight kilometers (five miles) distance from our hotel. We started walking slowly. On the way we stopped at a fruit shop and bought a bunch of eight bananas. We consumed two and put the remaining six of them in a plastic bag, to sustain us for the rest of the climb.

I was the one carrying the plastic bag. It was a lonely path with no one near us. The two of us walked hand-in-hand enjoying the cool breeze and lush green tall pine trees on the sides.

Suddenly I heard a screechy sound and felt a pull in my hand. For a while I did not realize what happened. After half a minute or so, it dawned upon me that the plastic bag had vanished from my hand! Someone had snatched it very fast, in a fraction of a second! We looked around – no one was visible. Suddenly we saw on a tree nearby, a monkey pulling out the bananas from the bag and eating cheerfully. When he saw us looking at him, the monkey showed us his teeth as if mocking us, or may be thanking us in his own way.

Here is another story of a visit to Vrindavan as told by my brother-in-law to me. He was walking along a crowded street to visit a temple. Suddenly he felt a mild thump on his back. He turned his head backwards. In a flash he felt some creature jump off from his shoulder and vanish. After a few seconds he realized his spectacles were no longer there. Quite surprised, he created a stir asking people around whether they had seen his spectacles fallen somewhere on the street. Someone stopped him and explained, "Don't worry. It is common here to find monkeys snatching the spectacles and waiting for the owner in one of the fruit shops. I suggest you look around for the monkey in the nearby fruit shops."

Yes! He found the monkey in one of the shops grinning at him, holding his specs! To recover the specs, he bought some bananas and offered to the monkey. The monkey obliged after eating a few bananas! This monkey business has actually become a tourist attraction in Vrindavan.

Okay, by now you must have guessed it. The President was advised not to wear spectacles in Vrindavan because monkeys there take pleasure in snatching spectacles from tourists!! They would not spare even the President of India with all his guards. But the President did not like to wear contact lenses. So he was taken around the temple lanes in a golf cart, with netting all around it!

No need to get alarmed about it. Normally monkeys are harmless, at worst they would snatch some food from you. You can ignore them or pamper them. On our way to Agra to see the Taj Mahal, we came across a troop of Langurs, long-tailed monkeys with black face, at an ancient shrine. My wife who loves nature and animals, felt at ease with the monkeys. While the rest of us including the kids were content to simply look at the monkeys from a distance, she made friends with them.

Deepali, friendly with monkeys; I too friendly, but from a safe distance

Afraid of so much proximity, I enjoy watching the postures and expressions of monkeys curiously watching us, sometimes imitating us. I often get close to a monkey (at a safe distance) and ask Deepali to shoot a photograph of me imitating their posture and expressions. As an old saying goes, "Monkey see; monkey do. Man see; man do."

Coming to Die in Australia

> *The phrase 'to die' has been the contention of many a joke on the Australian accent. Here is a real life story of a friend of mine caught unawares, as told in first person.*

I was visiting my son in Australia. I landed into some health problems. I got a checkup done. The results came the next day. The doctor told me that I needed to be admitted to the hospital for some further investigations to be done.

The next morning I got admitted in the hospital. The nurse took blood pressure and other vital data. A number of tests were done.

In the evening a new shift started and another nurse came in. The first thing she asked me after entering my room was "Have you come to die?" I got a shock. An interesting dialogue followed between the nurse and me.

Me: (mumbling) I have come for treatment.

Nurse: Have you come to die?

Me: (in a louder voice) I have actually come for treatment.

Nurse: Okay! Okay! But have you come to die?

Me: (In a bit of a panic, kept silent)

Nurse: (exasperated) Let me see the date in your registration card...... yes you have come *to die* only.

I shook my head realizing that 'today' in Australian accent sounded to me like 'to die', for which I had not entered the hospital under any circumstances. My mind went from desperation and fear to an immense and profound relief. Smilingly I explained to her my interpretation of 'Today' as pronounced by her in Australian accent. She gave a hearty laugh. That broke the ice immediately and she became a good friend during my short stay in the hospital.

"When you travel, strangers can become friends once you cross the barriers of inhibition."

7

Dining Around the World

> *"Sometimes you may have only two choices in the menu, take it or leave it."- Anon*

The Silent Admonition

I always enjoyed the typical finesse with which the food and drinks were served in formal dinners in England. At first people assemble at a hall adjacent to the dining hall around 7 p.m. The feast starts with aperitifs like Sherry or Gin & Tonic or wine along with a wide range of snacks to go with. With white glove service by uniformed stewards, the invitees break the ice as they sip the drinks. After an hour or so, a senior steward appears and announces in style – "Ladies and gentlemen, dinner is served".

You enter the dining hall and take a seat. The first round of dishes called appetizers, often grilled fish or prawn, are served along with white wine. The traditional prayer for a minute and you start to savor the dish, slowly chatting with your friends at a low volume. The next round is for the main dish. Dishes like Roast Beef, Roast Chicken or Cottage Pie are served with potatoes and vegetables and various kinds of sauces to pour over it. An array of red and white wines accompanies the main dish, served and tasted in style. The hum becomes louder and the dining hall becomes noisier by this time, as the inhibitions get drowned in a lot of wine.

By the time you are through with the main dish, it is around 10 o'clock. Then the dessert appears, mostly tarts of various kind, apple pie or ice cream with brownies. This is followed by a choice of cheeses with cream crackers and coffee. By the time you are through, it is nearing 11 p.m. The die-hards then go out together for a last round of fun at a nearby pub.

During my student days at Loughborough (around 1967), I experienced a major cross-cultural *faux pas*. It was a grand dinner with a lot of decorative candles lit on the table. The pre-dinner prayer was about to start. We all sat down solemnly along the dining table waiting for the prayer to start. Suddenly an Indian friend of mine, who was fond of smoking, took out a cigarette. Before I could stop him he bent his head forward towards a candle, the cigarette between his lips, and lit it!! To the diners around the table, mostly British, it was an anachronism.

But the British are well-known for guarded reactions. They all looked at my friend with an interesting expression, without a sound of exclamation or uttering a word. It was a mix of shock and disbelief combined with what we called a *Silent Admonition*".

Mind the Menu, Please!

I along with a colleague of mine were on a business tour to an oil rich country in the Middle East. After a few days of routine lunch and late evening dinner at a European restaurant of our hotel, my friend and I decided to have a good Indian dinner. We entered an Indian restaurant which seemed to offer a good range of Indian culinary fare. We took a window side table, with a dazzling view of illuminated glass-and-concrete structures outside.

The waiter brought the menu card. After a while he came to take the order. We ordered Chicken Dopiaza and were still looking at ordering another dish. But the waiter did not wait. We called him and told him that we had not finished ordering yet. We asked him to note down another dish for us – Mutton Rogan Josh. He gave us a strange look and rushed.

We stopped him again and ordered four pieces of *Rotis* (wheat pancakes roasted in earthen oven) to go with the dishes. He again gave us a strange look and asked if we were sure about ordering the *Rotis*. We answered in the affirmative. He looked at us in awe, shook his head and proceeded towards the kitchen. He left us wondering where the communication gap was!

After some time when he laid the meal on the table, we realized the meaning of the look on his face. A pan of ten inches diameter and four inches deep was placed in front of us, filled to the brim with Chicken Dopiaza in thick gravy. This was followed by a dish of Rogan Josh of the same size. Along with the dishes came twelve large and thick Rotis (around twelve inches in size). Eight of them free along with the two dishes we ordered, the waiter explained, and four more as per our order!!

Alas, when we finished, more than half of the food was left untouched! We were overconfident about ordering the food due to our familiarity with Indian cuisine. We did not care to look through the fine prints in the menu. It was a delicious dinner, left unfinished!

'Chicken Dopiaza' is an Indian dish. In Hindi 'Do; means 'two' and 'Piaz' means 'onion'. It is called Dopiaza because in this dish onions are added twice. First the diced chicken is cooked along with a large amount of chopped onions and Indian spices. Once ready, it is garnished with onions either fried brown or raw slices. There are other versions of it with shrimp or meat.

Literal translation of 'Rogan Josh' would mean 'Red Passion'. Lamb cooked with butter, yogurt and spices, it can be reddish in color due to liberal addition of dried red chilies. The passion is created by the flavor of special red chilies and spices.

Strictly as per Rule

Deepali and I were at Gosselies, Belgium, on an assignment of conducting a training program for a multinational company. The venue was at Charleroi Airport Hotel, a nice medium sized hotel, where we were accommodated by our client. The first day we had all our meals at the restaurant in the hotel only.

Our training program concluded in the late afternoon the next day. We decided to take a walk outside the hotel along the nearby streets to get a feel of the place and have a dinner out. It was a narrow street with two storied European style buildings. The sun was about to set. Occasionally we came across a few people who spoke only French. The place appeared to be a small conservative French speaking town without much of a life. Suddenly our day was enlivened up by a few children playfully riding scooter on the street.

The cheerful kids
It was difficult to locate a place for eating nearby.

Ultimately we found one restaurant and stepped inside. The moment we entered, we sensed that we had created some sort of tense environment inside. Most of the tables were full. All the diners were gazing towards us. In that small French speaking town perhaps they had never come across an Indian couple entering for dinner in that restaurant. They were looking at us as if some strange aliens had landed from the space.

We found an empty table nearby and got ourselves seated. Soon an elderly grim looking gentleman, perhaps the owner of the small restaurant, put the menu card on the table, without a word but definitely not politely. The menu card written in French was incomprehensible to us. My limited knowledge of French was alas not of much use! We were not very hungry and wanted a small size helping or split a dish into two between us. It was hard to explain as no one there seemed to understand English. The owner did not look very pleased to converse with us though he appeared to know a few words of English.

Suddenly we noticed a familiar word "Pizza" in the menu. We asked the owner what was the size of the pizza. He showed with his hand a size that was perhaps too much to eat for either of us alone. I said "One Pizza, two plates please". The owner seemed to be very upset with the request, picked up the menu card rudely and said "No! No! One Pizza one plate." With his gesture he appeared to be ready to throw us out if we insisted on "One Pizza, two plates please."

Although a small, self-owned restaurant, to the owner, 'A rule is a rule'. We said thank you very much and walked out. We walked back to the hotel to have our dinner in a friendlier environment, where no one objected when we shared a plate. It was in sharp contrast to the little children accepting us so easily and posing for a photograph with bright faces, on the way to that restaurant.

> *This incident left a bitter taste in an otherwise wonderful visit. But later we came to know that in some restaurants in Europe, if two people sit down at a table, both are expected to order. This rule is more applicable to a classy restaurant, where servings are small and quality is more important than quantity. But an average tourist restaurant doesn't care if you share a dish. This is an important cross cultural aspect – in a new place check if a meal can be shared.*

A Nice Cop in the Far East

[The story here is in first person as told by a friend of mine]

It was an evening of celebration after signing a contract. After enjoying an excellent feast of Dim Sum, poured down with some green tea and a lot of wine, I came out of the restaurant. I opened the door of my car parked by the side of the road. Before I could enter the car, I heard a grim voice, "You have parked in a 'No Parking' zone." Startled, I saw a traffic policeman standing with a not so friendly grin on his face. An occasional visitor to the country, I looked at him apprehensively, worried about the consequences. Then an interesting dialogue followed.

Policeman: Do you hear me? You have parked at the wrong place.

Me: I did not realize. I am a newcomer here. I just came from India yesterday.

Policeman: (After coming close to me and sniffing) You are drunk.

Me: No, I am not drunk. I only had a few rounds of red wine.

Policeman: I can prove that you are drunk.

Me: (Silent)

Policeman: You are fined.

Me: How much?

Policeman: One Thousand Dollars.

Me: I do not have so much money with me. Please give me the notice. I shall deposit tomorrow.

Policeman: Are you sure you want to pay the fine?

Me: Yes officer.

Policeman: (Repeats) Are you sure you want to pay the fine?

Me: Yes officer.

Policeman: (In a louder voice this time) Are you sure you want to pay the fine?

Me: (Realizing other possibilities) What else can I do?

Policeman: I shall give you a discount. Pay me 500 Dollars. Half price!

Me: (Alert now) I do not have so much. I spent all the

money I had in my pocket.

Policeman: You have a double offence. You have done wrong parking and you are drunk. I can't give you further discount, la!

Me: Then please give me the notice. I shall deposit tomorrow.

Policeman: How much money do you have?

Me: Only 100 Dollars officer.

Policeman: Then give me hundred (in a disgruntled voice).

Me: Here it is officer.

Policeman: Okay. I leave you this time. But next time you do wrong parking and get drunk, make sure that you have enough money with you!

A Peaceful Dinner

China, 1996 - It was a mission to secure a contract from a Korean multinational company. After a long period of marketing, it was in concluding stage of negotiation for a major contract. Vir and I landed in China on a bright and sunny morning with great anticipation and checked in at Holiday Inn, Beijing. After settling down in our rooms and a refreshing bath, we were ready for meeting the client for negotiation. There were frequent calls from the home office at New Delhi, where people were waiting in anticipation.

After eight hours of tedious discussions, all points were agreed upon, our fee was settled and the contract was ready. The moment we signed the contract, it gave us simultaneous feeling of relief and immense happiness.

Ours was a small start-up company and the order value was a game changer for us. We knew the moment we would give the news to our home office, we would be flooded with numerous calls and action plans. As CEO and a partner in the company, I took the liberty to spend one peaceful day at Beijing as a reward to ourselves after conclusion of the deal.

We sent a fax message to our office to confirm mission accomplished, "Tora, Tora, Tora. We are vanishing from the scene."

> *During the Second World War, the Japanese air force made a surprise attack on American naval base at Pearl Harbor. The base was completely destroyed. After achieving a total success, the Japanese Squadron Leader sent a coded message to their base "Tora, Tora, Tora" (Tiger, Tiger, Tiger).*

We switched off our phones. Then we quietly checked out of the hotel and checked into another hotel, without informing our office. No one except our families knew where we were. After moving around Beijing, which looked bright and glossy at night, we felt hungry. We entered a Chinese restaurant to savor authentic Chinese food. The manager came forward, greeted us politely and got us seated.

A slim and pretty Chinese waitress brought the menu

card. Browsing through the menu, one item caught our attention. It was "Bird's Nest Soup", an exotic name and also very expensive! Out of sheer curiosity, we ordered the soup. After placing the order for the soup, the girl came back to take the order for the main dish. In a short while the soup was served. It was tasty and a bit slippery to the tongue. We asked her what it was made of. Not very conversant with English she immediately went inside and brought out a small Chinese to English dictionary.

After turning some pages she wrote down "Swallow" on a piece of paper and handed to us. Wondering whether some swallows have been slaughtered to make the soup, we found her fumbling with the dictionary again. "Vomit" she wrote down now.

While we were trying to decipher the two words, we found her fumbling with the dictionary again. She shook her head and wrote down two more words with a smile of success - "Saliva" and "Nest". I immediately recalled the description given by my wife, a bird watcher, on how little swallows use their saliva with good binding quality to build a strong nest. So we were drinking a lot of birds' saliva! But I must say it was delicious saliva!

For the main dish we decided to go for Dim Sum. Hot Dim Sum dishes were being carted around the restaurant. It was easier to choose by the look of it. We picked up some attractive looking typical bite size Dim Sum dishes along with the accompanying sauce.

It tasted different from the kind of Chinese food served in India which is influenced by Tibetan and Nepalese cuisine with Indian spicy touch. But all of it went very well accompanied with Chinese tea. It was a very satisfying and peaceful dinner after vanishing from the scene of action on signing the contract.

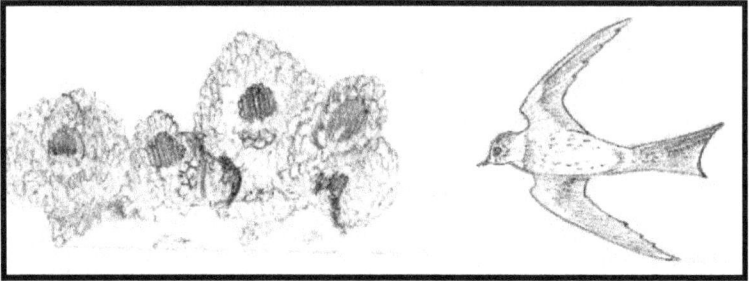

Barn Swallow and her nest

Eating Out in America

The most impressive part of eating out in the USA is the quality of food. It is uniformly good, generally top class. Perhaps only in Japan you can find anything comparable in the quality of food. In younger days, the first thing I used to order on arrival in America was a good steak, well done, with all the accompaniments of salad, baked potato with butter, cream or other fillings, along with a Bloody Mary. The freshness of every bit of food was always invigorating.

But the huge size of the servings always made me apprehensive while ordering. One of my friends explained that it was a practice to ask for a "box to go" for carrying back the left overs home. That is definitely very practical and eliminates the guilt of wasting, but not possible when on a business tour.

I found generally the waiters were polite and ready to explain the dish with fair detail to help choose the right dish. They are well trained and normally prepared to adapt the dish to the guest's requirement.

The food in America has been adopted from all continents. Mostly the restaurants offer European, Asian or Mexican cuisine. Americans have made a lot of interesting adaptations of such cuisine. But unfortunately they are not recognized as American Cuisine. I can think of fast food as an American contribution to the world cuisine. The fast pace of life in America created the need for food 'on the go'. Although most fast foods are referred to as 'Junk food', let us accept that munching a hamburger at the fast food outlets of MacDonald's or Burger King along with French Fries and a coke is definitely a pleasurable experience.

But being a believer in enjoying the food with as many of the five senses as possible, I have never been able to drink coffee, tea or Coca-cola from the tightly capped contraptions with a small slot at the top which all fast food joints serve. It is almost claustrophobic for me to drink anything from a container that does not allow access to all five senses. Of course it is convenient for the fast movers to pick-up a coffee of that kind from the drive-through counter and drink it while driving.

Personally, I always take my drink sitting in a restaurant, after uncapping the container disdainfully. Watching others drinking the suffocated coffee from the closed container, I realize that caught in the pace of life, people have forgotten to enjoy the smell and look of coffee while drinking.

Coffee uncapped at Starbucks

But fortunately the use of five senses to drink wine or beverages is still practiced in good restaurants. They still serve coffee in glistening china and serve drinks in glasses. The fun of a tiny bit of wine being poured in a sparkling glass held in the hand, the touch and feel of the sparkling glass, looking at it while swirling it, smelling it, tasting it for approval and then toasting it with tinkling sound of the glasses is still prevalent. That is enjoyment of food with all the five senses – touch, see the colors, smell the aroma, taste and then hear the tinkling sound. Yes, good dining is still practiced in good restaurants all over America. I hope someone will not come out with something called *'fast wine'* or *'wine on the go!'*

Drink Tequila the Mexican Way

Circa 1982 - it was a flight from Los Angeles to Mexico City. As the plane landed in Aeropuerto Internacional de la Ciudad de México (Mexico City International Airport), I was thrilled about my first visit to a Latin American country. I was on a business trip to look into potential for a technical collaboration with Pemex, a major oil and natural gas producing company in Mexico.

Immigration and baggage clearance at the airport was reasonably smooth. I went to the hotel booking counter and had my accommodation reserved at Holiday Inn near the airport. Surprise! Surprise! The tariff in US Dollars was much lower than what was being displayed on an electronic board. "The Mexican Peso is falling fast", the girl at the counter explained, "Your US Dollar rate is on the current value of Peso." I later came to know that some of the countries further down in South America had been undergoing faster drops in currency value in certain years. "Even the food bill in US Dollars might get cheaper by the time you finish your dinner," she said.

After freshening up with a shower and some food, I called my Mexican hosts. My meeting with Pemex was fixed at Villahermosa (pronounced Via-Moza), a town 750 kilometers away from Mexico City. I was informed that Pemex officials would meet me next morning and arrange for a car to take me to Villahermosa. The meeting with Pemex management was fixed at the site of a large gas processing plant near Villahermosa. It was an eight hour drive from Mexico city with a mid-way lunch stop.

Around 8 a.m. a young petite Spanish looking girl and a smart guy met me for breakfast in the hotel. She introduced herself as P.R.O. (Public Relations Officer) and her companion as her colleague in Pemex. "I always like to meet English speaking guests to sharpen my English," she said.

She got a chance to practice her English as we chatted about life in Mexico and India over breakfast! They had arranged a chauffeur driven car for me. "The car will drop you at a hotel in Villahermosa and a Pemex executive will meet you there. It is our General Manager's car. The driver is well trained and very dependable," she said. "Don't worry, the *bandolero* (Spanish for bandits) will not kidnap you on the way," said she, with a smile on her lips.

The drive was smooth along the way in the big and comfortable sedan. The chauffeur kept briefing me about interesting places on the way. We had a quick lunch at the historic city of Cordoba town and reached the hotel in Villahermosa around 6 p.m. A friendly looking gentleman greeted me at the hotel, "I am Carlos, your host from Pemex," he said. "You must be tired and hungry. I shall wait for you at the lobby. Have a shower and then we can have dinner together," he said in a reassuring voice. I was really hungry and the possibility of initiating an exploration of exotic Mexican cuisine added to my appetite. I was at the dinner table with Carlos within fifteen minutes. "What would you like for a drink?" asked Carlos. Between two of my favorite Mexican drinks – Tequila neat and Margarita, I chose the former. Carlos ordered Tequila for both of us along with some tidbits to go with it. Realizing that I was hungry he asked me about my choice of food. I gave him free hand to choose any good traditional Mexican food.

Tequila was served soon. Carlos showed me the traditional way of drinking tequila – first licking a bit of salt with lemon from the back of the palm and then gulping a shot of Tequila.

> *Agave tequilana, a cactus like plant known as blue agave, is fermented to produce tequila. Grown in Mexico, it has long succulent and spiky leaves and grows to about two meters in height. Fructose in the plant makes it suitable to produce alcoholic beverages. It has unique quality of preserving water by closing its breathing pores during day and breathing at night.*

Carlos looked like an Indian in appearance. When I told him that, he affirmed certain similarities of looks, cuisine and culture of Mexicans and Indians. He seemed familiar with Indian culture. Along with the shots of Tequila, we discussed about similarities of Burrito and Indian Roti rolls and similarities of chaos common to the third world countries. Soon some hot and exotic looking dishes were served. Carlos had ordered Pibli Pollo, a delicious main dish of chicken, cooked with red chilies, tomato and bitter orange juice. I enjoyed the spicy taste and the flavor. Bitter orange is the signature flavor of the dish.

For dessert, we had Caramel banana roll. It was banana with sprinkle of cinnamon and sugar, rolled in a tortilla and baked. With crispy exterior, soft banana inside plus the cinnamon and caramel flavor, it made a mouth-watering dessert.

We shook hands and called it a day. It was a typical Mexican handshake, where, after gripping the palm, the two people slide their hands upward to grasp each other's thumbs in a friendly way. Tired after the day's activities, I went back to my room and dropped dead into the bed.

Tequila is as neat a drink as Vodka with no morning blues. Early morning the next day I woke up refreshed ready for the day's engagements with Pemex.

Fish Head Curry in Singapore

During our stay in Singapore, we often heard from friends about a well-known Singapore delicacy – the fish head curry. An authentic fish head curry is traditionally prepared using Southern Indian spices. Normally snapper is the type of fish used for this dish. Being familiar with South Indian spices and the snapper being a tasty fish, we decided to give it a try in a restaurant, well-known for its fish head curry.

The Singaporeans originated from three main races – Chinese (born locally), Indians from southern India who migrated, and Malays, the original inhabitants of the Malaysian Peninsula. The cuisine in Singapore too is a mix of local Malays, Chinese and South Indian.

We went with our friends, ordered the fish head curry with other accompaniments and waited in anticipation. Then it arrived! It was in a huge bowl, about 14 inches in diameter and 8 to 10 inches in depth. The bowl was full of dark colored spiced gravy, and a large head of a fish popping out with its mouth open and the eyes staring at us. The fish head must have been around ten inches in length and eight inches wide with a fairly large girth. Both Deepali and I were not accustomed to seeing such a view of a fish delicacy. I was taken aback. Deepali looked at it with shocked expression and seemed to have lost her appetite altogether.

I realized Deepali had already given up the thought of even nibbling at it, leave aside eat it. I secretly pride myself as a gourmet. I did not want to give up. To be on the safe side, we ordered some other dishes. I nibbled at the huge head to keep my pride intact, before fish head lovers amongst the friends took over.

We Bengali Indians (meaning originating from the region of Bengal) are known to be fond of fish. We take pride in our cuisine, where no part of a fish including the fish head is spared. Fish head is added in different vegetable recipes to give an added flavor. Even it has a social significance. Prior to a wedding, the groom's family sends a freshly caught big sweet water fish in whole, nicely decorated with its head staring as a welcome gesture in honor of the bride. But those are different kind of fish heads of sweet water fishes, much smaller in size.

Even as a Bengali fish lover, I could not do justice to the fish head curry at Singapore.

Searching for a Typical Indian Meal

During my first visit overseas to England, I was astounded by the lack of knowledge about Indian cuisine. This in spite of a few hundred years of cross-cultural association between England and India! Many English friends used to ask me which curry were my favorite – Madras curry or Bombay curry or Delhi curry. These happen to be the names of places in India with the word curry added to it, and not the name of any authentic Indian dish.

I realized that most people associate Indian food with the single word 'curry'. They attribute all Indian cuisine to that one package of Indian spice called curry powder, easily available in any country and used in recipes of all kinds of Indian foods. Very few knew that numerous spices and herbs are used in Indian cuisine. One needs to pair different spices, from a few to a dozen varieties, to create dishes of different taste and flavor. The combination of spices varies depending on what type of vegetable or what type of meat or fish is being cooked. The complexity of Indian cuisine and the time it takes for a good recipe perhaps resulted in the short-cut called curry powder.

Things have changed now in England. During my stay in the late 1960s, 'Fish and Chips' was the most popular dish. Now with hundreds of Indian restaurants around, a recent survey showed that the most popular dish in England was 'Chicken Tikka Masala', an Indian dish modified to suit British taste.

Thank God, it was not called Chicken curry which it is not! I find just referring to any Indian dish as curry the most demeaning to Indian cuisine.

To add to the complexity and variety of Indian cuisine, the taste and flavor changes widely as one travels from North to South or East to West. There is nothing that I can call a typical Indian meal. Yes, there is something which is prevalent everywhere in India - the humble Indian *Thali* (or platter). It is a wholesome meal, typically having dishes of five flavors - bitter, salty, spicy, sour and sweet. As per Indian tradition, a perfect meal should be a balance of all these flavors. The dishes are served in small shiny stainless steel or copper *Katori* (bowls) placed around a single large plate, called *Thali* (plate). Traditionally, a fresh green banana leaf is used as *Thali*.

Staple food like rice and different types of breads (*rotis, naan,* etc.) along with sides of *paapad* (also known as Papadam), pickle and salad are served on the plate. And a range of local recipes are served in the bowls. It can be anything between half a dozen to a dozen items to savor. In many Indian restaurants specializing in *Thali*, the supply of food is unlimited for a fixed price. Every ten minutes a server will take a round seeing whose *Katori* is empty and approach to give it a refill. Beware, free refills may result in over eating!

Every Indian state has its own distinctive version of the *Thali*, suiting the local palate. While a Gujarati

Thali has to be purely vegetarian, Bengali *Thali* is not complete without at least one dish of fish and one dish of mutton or chicken or prawn, often all of them. I sign off with the picture of a *Thali* from Bengal, where my forefathers came from. Yes! You might have guessed it right. Bengal is the place the famous Royal Bengal Tiger comes from.

You may notice in the picture as you look at the dishes from right anti-clockwise, the full range of flavors from bitter to salty to sweet and sour is arranged in the *Katoris*. The sequence of eating is recommended to be in the same order.

A Thali from Bengal

Tea Diplomacy at Bhutan

This story was told to me by Shekhar Dutt, an eminent administrator and policy maker of the Government of India, as heard from one of his colleagues. His colleague was sent by the Indian government to serve as Military Advisor to the government of Bhutan. The story exemplifies typical style of slow and polite way of interaction in many Asian countries. It is an example how understanding of the culture helps in diplomacy and cross-cultural communication.

Cut off for centuries from the rest of the world, Bhutan, a small kingdom hidden in the Himalayas is known as The Last Shangri-La. These days it has opened up to a limited extent to the outside world, while fiercely guarding its culture of peace and harmony. It fervently protects its serene environment and simple way of life. It has always had close political, cultural as well as military ties with India.

It was one morning in the nineteen seventies. The Military Advisor posted there got a sudden call from his senior at New Delhi to look into certain developments at Thimphu, the capital of Bhutan. King Jigme Dorji Wangchuck had just passed away somewhere in Africa during a visit, after ruling Bhutan for 20 years. His last rites were to be performed the next day. There was an order by the Prime Minister that Indian military trucks should be off the road for the next few days. It was an abrupt and surprising order. The military advisor was asked to meet the Prime Minister to get a clear picture of the situation.

The Military Advisor easily got an appointment with the Prime Minister whom he knew well. He proceeded to his house at the scheduled time in the morning. He was received by a senior official. Soon the Prime Minister joined him. As they were seated, they were served typical Bhutanese tea – a strong black tea with a lot of lard.

He conveyed his condolences on the death of the King. Then they started talking about mundane things like mutual welfare, recapitulation of some past memories during his stay there and so on. They were sipping the tea during the discussion.

After fifteen or twenty minutes the minister waved his hands and some more tea was poured in their cups. Being familiar with Bhutanese culture, the Military Advisor knew that he had crossed the barrier and was welcome to continue their meeting.

Then the conversation hovered around world politics. They exchanged views on various issues around the world – economic, political and other issues while sipping the tea. Another fifteen-twenty minutes passed over this discussion. The minister waved his hand again. Some more tea was poured in their cups.

The Military Advisor knew this was a signal that now he could come to the point. He straightaway asked him why the Indian military vehicles have been ordered to be off the road stating that it has come as a surprise to the Indian government. The Prime Minister laughed heartily to relax the environment and explained -

"Tomorrow the mortal remains of our departed King will be brought from Africa," he explained. "We plan to carry his body in his favorite Jeep. The King loved his Jeep which he frequently used to go on his hunting trips. The Jeep will look very small compared to the huge Indian Army vehicles moving around in the streets of Thimphu. So we ordered all army vehicles, whether Indian or ours, not to come out on the streets of Thimphu tomorrow."

The Military Advisor heaved a sigh of relief. After exchanging some pleasantries he thanked the Prime Minister and bade him good bye.

> "Refresh the body with bath, refresh the mind with tea."- Japanese Proverb

8

The Indian Panorama

> *"Everyone I met who has been to India had a completely different experience to share." - Anon*

The Blind Men and the Elephant

The quote I started with reflects the multiplicity of India and the impossibility of capturing it by sharing some stories and experiences. Edward Luce, a well-known journalist, was asked what he found most attractive in India. His reply was "The complexity of India is most appealing."

Yes, trying to understand and describe India is like the story of blind men touching various parts of an elephant and describing the animal in different ways. More than 6000 years old civilization with migration of various races, invasions and refuge as safe haven, has created very diverse, often contradictory cultures.

During my schooling I had learnt about the diversity of India. But I had my first real exposure when I joined my alma mater, Indian Institute of Technology (IIT) way back in 1958. Being a premier institute, it drew students from all parts of India. On the first morning at my hall of residence I met someone with Mongoloid features and an unusual name, Bomber Nomgum. He was from one of the northeastern states, presently called Meghalaya. I learnt that people there love to use English words with powerful connotation as first name. Other popular first names were Clever, Bold etc. I was surprised to know that descent and inheritance in their society is matrilineal, so different from ours! I also got to know that for an Indian from the south, shaking head laterally means *yes* instead of *no*! Numerous cross-cultural experiences at IIT taught me to enjoy the diversity of India.

How to give a feel of such a diverse culture with some real life travel episodes? I have chosen to explore three themes out of many that highlight the harmony amidst such diversity.

The rural Indian and the urban Indian – The contradictions and harmony between simple rustic Indian and the modern high tech Indian.

The Indian railway journey – One can travel from any part to another part of India by train at a modest price, opening up numerous spontaneous human interactions during the journey.

The family and social life – Some unique facets of it, which any Indian visiting abroad misses.

The Rural Indian

Engineers versus Donkeys

The larger part of Indian population still lives in villages. The village folk are often poor and lacking in education. But the ancient wisdom prevails. Biswajit Das, an eminent hydraulic engineer who builds dams, has travelled and lived in some of the remotest corners of India. He had very interesting encounters with simple village folk and tribal people. Here is an interesting story as told by him, over a glass of wine.

For one of the hydroelectric projects I had to go to the Himalayan foothills in the North-East of India to a picturesque place called *Jaldhaka*. Surrounded by hills all around, lush green tea gardens and the Jaldhaka river from the Himalayan ranges flowing down to the valley, it is a place where you can feel the real magic of pristine beauty of mother nature.

The site was on a hill top (plateau) in a remote and dense forest area. First we had to build a guest house for the engineers there. We started a survey with gadgets like theodolites, staves and measuring tapes to build a road from the base of the hill to the top. The villagers had never seen such strange objects being used by people wearing hats and sunglasses. To the simple village folk in traditional dresses, we must have appeared like aliens from another planet.

For the first few days they came and watched us from a distance, wondering what was happening. Then came the Village Headman, a middle aged, burly looking tribal and asked my team men, "Who is your chief?" One of my team members pointed at me. I heard him muttering to his fellows in Nepalese language with a wry smile, almost mockingly, "Hah! He is too young to be a Chief. He is a kid!" I understood Nepalese language. I smiled at him.

The river at Jaldhaka

Then he looked at me and asked what was the hustle-bustle about. Our dialogue went somewhat like this...

Headman: What are you fellows doing?
I: (Wondering how to explain to a layman) We are working with these gadgets to establish the best route to build a road to the top of the hill.
Headman: (Loud Laughter) Ha Ha Ha Ha...
I: (A bit upset) Why are you laughing?

Headman: You guys are working so hard just to find the right route! We do it in a very simple way, just in a few hours.

I: What is the simple way, sir?

Headman: We bring a pair of donkeys, a male and a female donkey near the hill. We hold the male donkey here and take the female donkey to the top of the hill, at a location visible from below. They start braying at each other. Then we release the male donkey. The donkey takes the most convenient path round the hill as it climbs up to meet his mate. We follow the path and mark it up all the way. That becomes the best route to build the road.

Taken aback with the answer, I paused and asked, "But in this remote area, you may not get donkeys so easily. What do you do then?"

The Headman had never faced a question like that before. It was difficult for him to answer. He started scratching his head and fumbling for words. The village folk around were staring at him in anticipation. He perhaps thought he should display some respect for the engineers working so hard. They must be at least as useful as donkeys.

Then he came up with an answer with the innocence typical of simple village folk, "Okay! Okay! When we don't get donkeys, we call engineers."

I did not know what to say after this gem of an answer!

The Truth and Nothing But the Truth

It was way back in the 1950's. My father was posted as a judge in the town of Dumka in eastern India. The place was predominantly populated by *Santhal* tribe. Though I was a child, I still have fond memories of the place. An iron ore rich area, the soil there is red in color. We used to enjoy the red dust storms before the monsoon rains.

> *The mountains and forest rich areas of India are inhabited by different tribes, called 'Adivasi' meaning 'the original inhabitants'. They are a sizable 10% of India's population. Some of them still maintain their ancient culture and tend to shun modern civilization to lead a simple life. Many are still dependent on hunting, agriculture and fishing for their livelihood. They have their unique art and culture - dancing is an integral part of their culture.*

Santhal girls in dance attire

My father used to tell us interesting incidents about the simple nature of *Santhals* and their dependability as witness. "They would never lie and tell only the truth," he used to say. I do not remember all the stories. Here is one I have put together, based on whatever bits and pieces I still remember.

A Santhal male called Birju had committed a very brutal pre-planned murder. A trial was on in the court of law. In India, death by hanging can be the ultimate punishment in what is called 'rarest of rare cases' of brutal murders. The murder Birju had committed was brutal and gory enough to fall in that category.

The defending lawyer had called many of Birju's close relations as witnesses for the defense. All his family members were very fond of Birju and pleaded with the lawyer to save him. It seems Birju did it due to a deep sense of hurt on something related to family honor. He had earlier expressed his intention to his close ones to kill the person. They had been trying to pacify him. But one day Birju murdered him in a fit of rage. Birju's brother who loved him dearly and a few others relations, were present in the scene of murder. It was so abrupt that they could not stop him.

Aware of the tribal commitment to tell the truth, the defending lawyer told them that the only way to save the man from death penalty would be to tell the truth but not the whole truth.

The defense lawyer rehearsed with them to maintain the following lines of defense ...

- The room was dark and they did not clearly see the action during the murder.

- Maintain that it all happened in the heat of the moment due to grave provocation by the deceased and it was not pre-meditated.

The defendant's brother was the first witness. A poor street vendor, he appeared in the witness box looking sad and uncomfortable at the glare of the lawyers and the judge. The cross examination went this way –

Defending Lawyer: Were you present at the room of the deceased when the murder took place?
Brother: Yes.
Defending Lawyer: Was the room dark?
Brother: No.
Defending Lawyer: (Not happy with the answer) Was the light in the room dim?
Brother: Yes.
Defending Lawyer: Did the deceased shout at and abuse your brother?
Brother: Yes.

There was some more questioning on the details on the kind of abuses the deceased hurled on Birju, to which the witness replied truthfully. The defending lawyer concluded by stating that all this happened in a fit of sudden rage without any prior intent to murder, due to the barrage of abuses hurled on the defendant.
The prosecution lawyer then started his interrogation of Birju's brother.

Prosecution Lawyer: Why did you go to meet the deceased?

Brother: I did not go to meet him. My brother had gone there to meet him.

Prosecution Lawyer: Why were you present there?

Brother: The moment I heard that my brother had gone to meet him, I rushed there.

Prosecution Lawyer: Why did you rush there?

Brother: To stop him from killing the deceased.

Prosecution Lawyer: How did you guess he would try to kill him?

Brother: He was very upset with the deceased. He felt deeply humiliated and told us of his plans to kill him in revenge. We had been trying to pacify him.

Prosecution Lawyer: How far were you from your brother and the deceased when the incident occurred?

Brother: We were sitting close together.

Prosecution Lawyer: Was the room lighted?

Brother: Yes, a kerosene lantern was there.

Prosecution Lawyer: Was the lantern close enough to see each other clearly?

Brother: Yes.

Prosecution Lawyer: Did you see your brother stabbing the deceased fiercely several times?

Brother: Yes.

No guesses on whether the verdict was 'guilty' or 'not guilty'. Though he knew the fate of the defendant, the witness could not divert a bit from the truth.

Yoga at the Himalayas

It was the summer of 2011. In Delhi the temperature had soared to over 40 degrees Celsius (104 ºF). My wife, Deepali, and I always love to escape to the cool and pristine environment of the Himalayan Mountains in some small habitats known as "Hill Stations." The surroundings present another facet of rural India.

Getting a good accommodation in the mountains during summer is always difficult, unless booked well in advance. One of our friends, a follower of a sect preaching *Sahaja Yoga* (*a way for meditation and self-realization*) came to our rescue. He arranged for our accommodation in their *Ashram (dwelling place for the followers)*. It is located in Naddi, a village at a height of 2200 meters (7000 feet) above sea level in the Himalayas.

The Himalayan ranges cover the entire northern border of India, with a spread of over 2000 miles from Myanmar in the east to Pakistan in the West. The entire region of the Himalayan ranges and its foothills offer some of the best tourist destinations in the world. During the colonial rule, the British government officials used to escape there from the heat of the plains during the summer. They fondly termed the mountain habitats as 'Hill Stations'. Now the Indian middle class, 'yuppies' and the rich make it a point to rush to the hill stations during the heat of summer.

An overnight train journey followed by a drive of five to six hours along scenic narrow winding roads lead us to the doorstep of the *ashram*. The room was spartan but reasonably comfortable. There was no access to TV or cellphone which are supposed to be not conducive to meditation. From the window of our room in the *Ashram,* we got a magnificent view of the snow clad Dhauladhar mountain with its peak about 5,640 meters (18,500 feet) high.

View from the window

During the mornings and evenings we would participate in the prayers and practice of *Sahaja Yoga*. Sahaja Yoga means "Simple Yoga" (meditation). The rest of the time we used to take long treks along the mountain trails. It was real rural India with simple people living in the pristine environment.

Sahaja Yoga is a simple technique of meditation and a new religious movement founded by a spiritual lady Late Mataji Nirmala Devi. It starts with sitting quietly and creating a feeling of forgiveness by chanting, *"I genuinely forgive all who affected me; I forgive myself; Oh God, forgive me for all my mistakes."*

It is followed by some simple rituals like touching various parts of our own body, touching the earth which is supposed to absorb the negatives and raising a hand to receive the positives from God. Both Deepali and I, during the guided meditation sessions really got a feeling of what was described as 'cool breeze' from the top of the head.

Once during a prayer session in the morning, some school children were singing a prayer on the same theme. A strange surcharged feeling passed through our body. When we said this to the preacher, he explained that the children have pure souls and their prayers create stronger vibes.

The disciples who gathered there were simple people, from all over India and other countries. The preachers, mostly volunteers, were not so conversant with English. A lot of foreigners used to come, whom the volunteers found difficult to communicate with. After a few days we could understand the basic principle of *Sahaja Yoga*. One afternoon some Spanish tourists, who spoke English, visited the *Ashram*. With the barriers of language as well as accent, the volunteers there found it difficult to explain the philosophy of Sahaja Yoga. Deepali and I immediately took over and started explaining the philosophy to the visitors. Although a novice on *Sahaja Yoga*, we could convey the message of self-realization through forgiveness. One of the Spanish visitors made an interesting comment –"I find it most difficult to forgive myself." The secret of good living perhaps lies in being at peace with self!

The Austrian Girl

It was one of our long treks along the mountain trail from Naddi to McLeodgunj, abode of Dalai Lama, the Tibetan spiritual leader. We met a lone European girl walking along the same trail. We started walking together and chatting.

She was from Austria. She often came to Naddi and stayed for long periods. She had made friends with many of the locals and was staying with one of her friends.

"Do you feel unsafe while moving around alone?" Deepali asked her.

"No," she said, "I have been coming for last so many years but never faced any problem living as a single girl. I always carry a 'Red Chili Spray' with me, but never faced a situation to use it."

Deepali asked what brought her to India so often, "Was it Spirituality? Or was it in search of peace? Or was it the charm of the Himalayas?" The answer was 'no' to all that. Her reply was interesting.

"People here are simple and friendly compared to Europe. They are interested in each other and I feel well accepted. People genuinely interact with me. But in Austria it is a far more individualistic life," she said. She made it clear further, "People in Austria live in their own limited sphere with the attitude – *Let me be on my own and so be you.*" Here, she said, she found genuine friendship of people which was beyond any professional or any selfish motivation.

The trek was refreshing with cedar and pine forests around, view of snow-clad mountains and ancient temples and churches to stop by. Her simple airs and friendly chat made the one hour trek to McLeodgunj a pleasant experience.

Trail to McLeodgunj

The Urban Indian - The Street Scene

The street scene in Delhi represents the complete microcosm of the urban Indian society. Like any developing economy there is huge migration from countryside to the city, making Delhi one of the largest cities in the world. This coupled with the propensity of many Indians of not sticking to the rules, often leads to chaos on the streets. Still there is a strange harmony and peace within the chaos. "We thrive in chaos," someone commented proudly. After the stories of rural India, I thought the street scene of Delhi best describes the urban Indian.

The traffic on the roads is very complex. From the poor to the middle class to the rich, each has his own way of transportation, from BMWs to tiny cars, ubiquitous three wheelers called '*auto*'s, latest battery powered avatar of '*auto*' known as *e-rickshaw* (i.e. electric rickshaw), bikes, pedal rickshaws, bicycles and push carts. Add to that, the pedestrians spilling over from the pavements, where the space gets increasingly occupied by street vendors displaying their wares. It perhaps reflects the frantic competition to be one up in a fast growing economy and modernization. A poor migrant from a village driving a pedal rickshaw strives to get into the next upper strata of *Auto or e-rickshaw.*

In the competition to occupy the available space, the driving habits of people of Delhi are particularly aggressive. Watching the cars merrily honking their way ahead on the streets, an American friend of mine made one interesting observation! Indians honk on the streets just to announce, "I am here, about to occupy the road space near you." For most part, there does not seem to be any other reason.

To an outsider, if he watches the traffic standing on a pedestrian bridge, it would look like a random movement of innumerable vehicles of all kinds spilling into the road. Watching the people cross the road amidst the chaotic traffic, he would expect an accident any moment. But it does not happen! Why? The reason lies in perhaps a description of the street scene made by a blogger – 'Harmonious chaos'.

View from a pedestrian overbridge

The blogger from abroad nicely explained "It is communication and understanding between the drivers of all kinds of vehicles coupled with will to accommodate each other." It can be audio as well as visual – even silent understanding from experience. The first method is loud and clear audio, that is honking. Depending on the intensity and frequency it conveys certain things. A single peaceful tweet may just mean, "Beware, I am here, in case you have not seen me." A few short tweets may mean, "Look at the mirror. You are treading into my path." Repetitive long impatient honking may mean, "I am in a hurry and I am a bully. Give me way to overtake you."

A typical visual method is flashing the headlight a few times in a narrow passage to warn a car approaching from the opposite side. It means, "Slow down and give way to me." The silent understanding borne out of experience is also important. For example from the body language of a pedestrian or cyclist crossing the road at odd places one can get a clear idea whether one should move on or brake and let him go. To a learner, golden rules to follow are, learn to drive slow, stop whenever in doubt, let trucks, buses and bicycles have their way and start honking if you are scared!

The pedestrian scene is equally diverse. I remember when *burqa* was banned in one of the European countries, there was a heated discussion on the topic in an Indian TV show. A Muslim gentleman proudly commented, "We are lucky to be in India. Here an executive in a suit, a Muslim lady in *burqa,* a girl in a skirt and a barely dressed *Fakir* can be seen walking on the same street, without anyone batting an eyelid."

Occasionally stray animals can catch you by surprise. My nephew's Japanese fiancé on her first visit to India, saw some cows ruminating in the middle of a busy road. "Wow! What are the cows doing here?" she asked shocked. "They are having a meeting," replied my nephew with a deadpan expression!

But true to the diversity of India, beyond the squalor and chaos, streets of Delhi provide some unique sights and beauty. While driving one comes across several beautiful neat tree lined avenues. Many are colorful with dazzling red bougainvillea, tall Gulmohar trees (Flame tree) and golden Amaltas (Indian Laburnum) flowering with bright colors. Add to that the variety of modern glossy buildings and numerous ancient monuments spread around.

The ancient... a 700 year old fort

And the new ... a modern office block

The contrasting street scene reflects a harmonious living in urban Indian society. It truly represents the diverse cultures, the poorest to the richest strata of society and migrants from villages to suave urbanites all living amidst harmony.

The Romance of the Indian Railway

In my early childhood, I used say that I wanted to become an engineer. The only catch was that I did not know what an engineer really meant. To me it meant a railway engine driver. The chug-chug steam engine of those days cooing through the green fields and mountains fascinated me. Though eventually I became an engineer of the kind defined in the dictionary, the railway in India still fascinates me.

The railways are so well encompassing in the lives of Indians, covering all major towns and cities in its vast stretches! It is one of the world's largest railway networks covering about 65,000 km (over 40,000 miles) and has nearly 7,500 stations. It transports over 9 billion passengers annually, besides billions of kilograms of freight - anything from common merchandise to all kinds animals, huge machinery and construction materials.

The best way to see and understand India is by taking a long journey by train. Often, within an hour of getting seated in the coach, co-passengers from all walks of life who are strangers to start with, become good friends. You start sharing your experiences, food, advice, gossip, discussing cricket, politics and everything else that makes journeys on trains in India so fascinating even for grown-ups.

Let us start our journey with one of such experiences of friendly interaction with strangers.

The Friendly Couple on the Front Seat

A niece of ours recalls an interesting incident from her early childhood days. It happened perhaps when she was six years old or less, while traveling by train with her parents. She still remembers the incident although it happened more than twenty years ago. Here is how the story goes.

It was a longish, overnight journey from Kolkata (known as Calcutta those days) to Patna, a fairly large town. There was a Sikh couple seated facing them in the same compartment. All of them soon became friendly. It appeared that they were traveling up to a station which was further ahead of our niece's destination - Patna.

Along with a friendly chit chat, the couple opened a large packet of peanuts and offered it to other co-passengers. They started breaking the shells, eating the nuts and throwing the shells on the floor. Our niece, a little girl then, was getting quite disturbed seeing the floor getting strewn with groundnut shells. "Why don't you tell them not to throw the shells on the floor?" she whispered to her parents.

The Sikh couple noticed that. They thought that she wanted some peanuts and offered it to her. But she was not interested.

"What is she looking for?" asked the Sikh gentleman after a while, looking quite concerned.

Her parents frankly explained the problem to them.

The couple acknowledged and immediately cleared up the mess. At that point, the Sikh lady took out a ball of wool and a pair of knitting needles and started knitting something. Friendly chit chat between the two families continued while sharing the dinner. After a while, our niece and her parents fell asleep, while the lady continued her knitting.

In early hours of the morning, the train started slowing down to halt at our niece's destination – Patna. The Sikh lady had finished knitting by that time. As our niece and her parents were getting ready to disembark, the Sikh lady handed over a nice packet to our niece, gave her a hug and said, "Good bye." Our niece's mother opened the packet. Surprise! It was a nice woolen cap which she had been knitting!

A halt at a railway station

Traveling the Third Economy Class

The Indian railway connects the entire country serving the poorest as well as the rich. As a result, the long distance trains provide different levels of comforts at different prices – air-conditioned (AC), non-air-conditioned, sleeper berths, seating (reserved and not reserved).

Types of sleeper berths in Indian Railways-

1A (First AC): The coach divided into several cabins with doors opening to a common corridor. Four or two persons per cabin, it is spacious and comfortable.

2A (Second AC): More compact, more berths in the same space, no doors, privacy by curtains.

3A (Third AC): 3-tier arrangement of berths

3E (Third Economy): As 3A but not Air-conditioned.

Traveling in First Air Conditioned Class termed 1A or 1st AC allows for a comfortable journey with perks like your bed being made and food served by an attendant. Since decades we have been traveling in 1st AC. But during student days and the early part of my career we could not afford to travel in 1A Class. We used to enjoy traveling in Third Economy class (3E) which was not air-conditioned. Even today after so many years, we and our children who now live in America, cherish the memories of travel in 3E.

Before writing this piece on railway travel, we exchanged views with our children over internet chats. They recalled an interesting incident when we all were traveling together in 1A. After a while they got bored with the monotonous luxuries of traveling AC First Class and walked all the way through the many air-conditioned coaches to the 3E non-air conditioned coach at the end of the rake. After a few hours they came back – refreshed and re-charged. There was unanimous agreement amongst us that travel in 3E captured the real fun of traveling by train in India. The points that came out during the chats and later discussions are -

- The rhythmic chugging and clinking sound of the train was music to the ears. The sound of the train is so muffled in today's air-conditioned coaches!
- Friendly co-passengers, endless discussions, sharing of meals, singing and playing cards. The beautiful feeling of fresh air rushing in through the windows.
- As the train stops at a railway station, the chanting of the *Chaiwalah* (tea vendors) selling tea, *Chai Garam, Chai Garam* (Hot Tea, Hot Tea).
- Then buying the hot tea served in a *Kulhor* (small disposable earthen pot) through the window.
- If the stop is long, vendors entering the coaches to sell books, magazines, children's toys, cold drinks and what not.
- The meals we used to buy served in a plate made of dried leaves stitched together. Oh God! Now they are replaced by plastic cups and plastic plates!

The memories were endless!

Plastics replacing eco-friendly Kulhor

Our daughter, Rini, later composed a nostalgic poem on train rides, a part of which goes....

The journey begins with excitement in the air
With a clanking sound and the whistle loud and clear
We settle in the seats that we sometimes need to share
When in the third sleeper, whether or not we care.

Excitement and fun, an adventure of a kind,
Not for the faint at heart, etched forever in my mind.
People engrossed, in chatting and laughing,
Stories from every walk of life, come pouring.

When you want a break, from endless talks that abound
You feast your eyes on scenes, changing all around
And suddenly in the middle of nowhere, we stop
No one knows why, excited mulling in the air ...

Some start to step down, to walk for a bit
The whistles finally calls, for all to get in
The train takes off, this time at a speed
And life buzzes again, in the train within.

This time when we stop, it's a station.. yay!!
More sounds to add to the symphony we play
The porters called coolie, in their turbans and red robes
Carrying luggage to and fro, the start of chaos

UTPAL K DUTTA

Vendors selling chai, puri, aloo, even toys
And books for all, men, women, girls and boys
Passengers happy to buy, whatever the choice
To satisfy their stomachs, and fuel their voice.

Back to the comfort of the sights that whizz by
Some mountains green, in the distance loom high
Birds perched on cables, crops that sway in the breeze
With tiny yellow flowers, dancing with ease

And soon it is time, for some rest at night
The hum starts to dim, and we turn out the light
With it's rhythm of comfort, the train rocks all to sleep
The ride gets over, but with memories to keep.

It was like time travel to the past with interesting memories to dwell on. All these were so nostalgic that it reminded me of a poem by Robert Louis Stevenson of bygone days of train journey titled "From a Railway Carriage" which beautifully described the views from a railway carriage. Some parts of the poem I still remember....

"Faster than fairies, faster than witches,
Bridges and houses, hedges and ditches;
......
......
......
......
Here is a cart runaway in the road
Lumping along with man and load;
And here is a mill, and there is a river:
Each a glimpse and gone forever!"

184

The Friendly Railway Engine Driver

It was sometime around the late 1990s. Our son, Arup, was studying at a university far away from the city of Delhi, where we lived. It took an overnight journey by train to reach there. During each vacation or short holiday breaks, all the students from Delhi used to travel back to Delhi to be with their parents. With so many students traveling on the same days, sometimes it used to be difficult to get reservation of sleeper berths. On one of his many trips to Delhi, Arup ended up with his gang of friends in a crowded un-reserved coach next to the engine.

After several hours of smooth ride, the train stopped at a nondescript railway station. It was waiting for a long time for the green signal to proceed. There was some problem in the railway track and the train was to be diverted to another route. Arup got down and bought tea served in a Kulhor, a small reddish clay pot, so common in the railway stations those days.

While sipping tea, he started a polite conversation (what our children used to call PC) with a person standing close to him. It all started with a goods train speedily crossing the passenger train standing at the station.

"That's unusual," said Arup, "Why should a goods train be given priority over the passenger train?"

"Yes! Just look at it! These days they do not care about the passengers," the person replied wryly.

"Where are you going to?" he asked Arup. Soon the signal on the track turned green.

"Would you like to join me at the railway engine?" he asked Arup.

Arup realized that he was the engine driver. He gladly agreed. Arup told him that as a mechanical engineering student, he would love to look at the gadgets and systems in the engine. They both got into the engine. There was an assistant to the driver in the same engine cabin. The train started and as it rolled on, the driver explained the controls to Arup. After a while, the driver opened a flask and poured some coffee for all three.

"My wife at home made this coffee for me," he explained. Although not so fond of coffee, Arup enjoyed the luxury of drinking nice and hot homemade coffee along with good company.

After some time, the train had a scheduled stop. "You better go back to your coach now. After this station, a major junction station will come, where there will be a lot of inspection," said the driver.

It was a great first-hand experience of learning about the railway engine from a friendly railway engine driver, who knew it in and out.

Alas! With the increasing terrorism all around the world, such pleasant encounters are not possible any more.

The Social Life - Snapshots

No Formalities

Deepali and I were returning home after shopping. It was a kind of a longish shopping spree which makes me tired. I wonder how women manage to shop without ever getting tired! And when I am tired I get an irresistible urge for a hot cup of tea with some tidbits. We were driving along a residential area where our close friends Subir and Neha lived. I picked up my cell-phone and called Subir. The moment my friend picked up the phone, I asked him where he was and what he was doing. Sensing that everything was normal, I announced that in a few minutes we were dropping in! We were warmly welcomed and had a great time chatting together at their home with hot tea and more than just tidbits. Such surprise visits between friends and close relations are very common. It does not need prior calling, checking availability and fixing time to meet except on formal occasions. People take each other for granted with pleasure and the word 'Thanks' is not often uttered between close ones. If I keep saying 'Thank you' to my wife for all that she does for me, she would wonder whether I am terribly upset with her and vice versa.

Starting a conversation with a stranger is commonplace in India, which foreign visitors sometimes find intrusive. I did a search of blogs on impressions about India by tourists. One conclusion I made was that those who overcome the fear of the crowd and feel at ease with strangers, start enjoying it. Those who get tensed up seeing 'friendliness' from strangers, get a culture shock and keep getting worried about 'loss of personal space'.

Secularism – The Indian Interpretation

It was sometime around November, 2007. It was a day we were celebrating an annual Hindu festival – *Bhai Dooj*. Bhai Dooj celebrates the bond between a brother and a sister. On this day, sisters touch their brother's forehead with a finger dipped in Sandalwood paste and pray for their good health and long life. Deepali had invited her brother along with her adopted Muslim brother with his family. She also invited her cousin with his American wife. After the ceremonies and a dinner at home, we had a session of music where all contributed with their voice. Our Muslim friend's daughter sang a hymn for the Christian wife of Deepali's cousin – a typical example of multi-religious bonhomie in a Hindu festival.

India is a land of festivals – religious, social and many other types. Some of them are unique in their own way. Indians are 'game' for any festival which promises and encourages eating, drinking, merrymaking and bonhomie between people.

I noted a major difference in the interpretation of secularism in India and some of the western countries. In the West, secularism means avoidance of religious celebrations in public and keeping religious expressions private. In India it means celebration of all religious festivals by all communities - loud and clear. Christmas here is celebrated with greater fervor than in Vatican City. During Eid, Hindus and Muslims greet each other "Eid Mubarak." Hindu families visit homes of Muslim friends, hug each other and enjoy the special dishes cooked at home – no invitation needed. Hindu festivals like Diwali symbolizing victory of good over evil is celebrated with decorative lights and crackers in full fervor by all. That is the kind of secularism Indians aspire for.

But aberrations do occur. The multi-religious bonhomie sometimes gets shattered when religious passions are whipped up by politicians to meet their own selfish ends. The silent majority starts suffering due to a rabid minority.

Pretensions in the Land of Gandhi

Gujarat is a state where Mahatma Gandhi, one of the outstanding leaders of the world, was born. During the 1990s I used to often visit Vadodara, a thriving and prosperous business center in the state of Gujarat. It is a very cultured city of nice polite people and perhaps among the safest cities in the world. It is one of the very few cities in the world where young girls move around in two-wheelers alone, fearless even in desolate streets late at night.

A vegetarian and teetotaler, Mahatma Gandhi led a simple austere life. Hence as a mark of respect, Gujarat is designated a *dry state*. You need a special permission or doctor's certificate to buy a drink. But strangely I found that the locals of the state, known as the Gujaratis, have as much love for Scotch whisky and red wine as in any other state of India. Most of the parties I attended in this dry state had a good choice of alcoholic drinks served.

Once on a business trip alone way back in the nineteen nineties, I decided to host an evening get together with business associates. I found a well-stocked store of drinks with the sign "Permit Room" at the basement of the hotel I had checked in. I asked the salesman for a few bottles. He said I had to get a "permit" from the police to buy a drink. Seeing me taken aback, he told me not to worry. He directed me to an adjacent room in the basement, where I met a policeman, authorized to give permits. The sedentary life of sitting in a basement room and issuing permits had made him plump and pot-bellied. He gave me a blank stare and handed over an application form for drink permit written in Hindi language.

Once I started to fill the form, I got a shock! The first item in the form was worded *Sharabi Ka Naam*. The literal translation of this means "Name of The Drunkard." It fitted with the stereotyped concept of certain conservative sections in the Indian society, who believed if you drink, you have to be a drunkard.

It reminded me of various stages of drinking humorously defined by our son, Arup. These were, "Stage-1 Cheerful, Stage-2 Noisy, Stage-3 Tipsy, Stage-4 Random motion and Stage-5 Totally peaceful." Obviously the application form for permit implied that if I have to buy a drink, it must be for reaching Stage-5 to attain a peaceful *Nirvana!*

The next item in the form was still more horrifying for me. It said, "Sharabi Ke Baap Ka Naam." Literally translated it means, "name of drunkard's dad." Normally most application forms in India, require father's name also. The equivalent civilized Hindi is *'Pita Ka Naam'* meaning father's name. They perhaps decided that the word *Pita* (Father) is too good a word for a drunkard's dad. It was quite obvious that whoever drafted the form, thought a person who enjoys a few pegs of whisky is the worst possible sinner. Anyway I surrendered my pride to write the name. There were several such questions on family history which I completed, signed the form and handed it over to the policeman.

But the last shock was still pending. The policeman reviewed the form and told me that it still did not give enough reasons to issue a permit for drinks. "Please write the following statement," he dictated, "I am an alcoholic and for my survival it is essential for me to have alcohol."

Thus with all the humiliation completed, I was allowed to buy any number of bottles. I bought some bottles for my friends as well as for my evening party. Procuring drinks is easy for the locals, I was told. The source could be a friendly doctor prescribing alcohol on health grounds or the omnipresent friendly bootlegger.

That was the scene in the nineties. Now one can apply online for 'permit' to buy drinks in Gujarat. I found that the online forms are simpler and in more polished language!

Does a 'dry' state concept work anywhere? On a dry state elsewhere in the world, BBC News magazine (21 March 2012) reports, "Far from ending corruption and vice, as opponents of the 'demon rum' had hoped, prohibition led to an unprecedented explosion in criminality and drunkenness." The story repeats everywhere.

Lost and Found

In the past, say seventy years ago, Delhi was a much smaller city reputed as abode of cultured and polite people. But rapid growth and huge migration from other states gave it cultural and socio-economic transformation. Delhi after the late sixties earned a reputation as a rough and rude city. Here is a story in 'first person' by our daughter from her college days in the nineties, which challenges this stereo-typing of Delhi.

An incident comes to my mind from my college days. I used to take the *University Special bus* of the city bus system from home to Delhi University and back. It was over one hour ride to the University area, enlivened with chatter of young boys and girls.

On way back one fine afternoon I got down from one such 'university special' near about my home. As I saw the bus going by, I realized I had left my precious denim jacket in the bus. Yes, bordered with fine embroidery it was my most expensive piece of clothing at the time. I had spent time and money to buy it. I was not ready to let it go easily. I decided to track down the bus immediately and retrieve it.

I looked around and spotted an 'auto', the ubiquitous three wheeler scooter driven public transport found all around Delhi. That was the only auto around. I rushed towards it but I was too late. Another lady had already 'claimed' it. I explained my situation. I told her that I needed to track down the bus somehow and fast enough. "Jump in," said the lady, "I shall drop you at another auto stand nearby."

The auto-stand where she dropped me was full of autos, but with no drivers in them. It was lunch hour. They had all gathered together and were having a leisurely lunch around a cart carrying street food. I addressed the group of men, and asked if anyone was willing to help me out with tracking the bus down and retrieving my stuff. One of the drivers left his meal and volunteered. And he became my most helpful buddy for the rest of the adventure.

We started heading down the road, not knowing where to go. Every time we saw a Delhi Transport bus coming from the other direction, the auto driver and I would wave our hands vigorously and hail the bus driver. The bus would stop in the middle of the road. I would get off from the auto and cross over to the driver to ask him if he had any idea which bus depot my university special was headed to. This happened a few times with the bus driver politely stopping the bus, patiently hearing me out and trying to help. Finally one of the drivers suggested we go to Kalkaji bus depot, the nearest bus terminal. We rushed to the Kalkaji bus depot.

I talked to the bus drivers and the crowd around there too, who were all very polite and willing to help. We were directed inside to the enquiry counter. We were told that the university special terminates in another depot, Okhla bus depot, which was further down.

With the help of some directions for Okhla bus depot, we reached there. It seemed like a peak lunch hour going on in front of the bus depot. The road was full of food stalls, carts with street food and totally crowded, with the bus drivers too eating after completing their rounds. And the bus depot was huge! Again the auto driver and I started talking with different groups of people. It was the same pattern for me. Every person politely listened, and in fact started asking others around too if anyone knew where the driver or conductor of that University Special bus was. It was really chaotic with the huge crowd, and chances seemed low of being able to locate anyone.

I was directed to the lost-and-found section of the bus depot, but my jacket was not there. I was heading back to the auto and was thinking of giving up. Suddenly I saw somebody running towards us from inside the depot. It was the same conductor who was in the University Special I was travelling!! Apparently the news had spread like wildfire in the depot. The moment he heard about us he came running to track us down. He said that the jacket was safe and he had not taken it to the lost-and-found yet. He asked us to wait while he got it from the bus. In ten minutes he brought the jacket to us, all intact. I thanked him and everyone around. Mission Accomplished!!

The auto driver finally dropped me home. I asked him how much I needed to pay him. He had not turned on the meter in a hurry. He was not very interested in charging me, and said I could give him whatever I wished. Those days the fare if metered for all the travel would be around Fifty Rupees (One Dollar). I did not have much money on me. I went inside home and took one or maybe two hundred (a few Dollars) from my mother, and gave him that. I thanked him from the core of my heart before he left, but unfortunately did not think of asking his name.

Often there is profiling of a community or race or profession. Delhi people, particularly bus drivers or other less educated people in Delhi are profiled as rough and rude – better to avoid interaction with. I must have talked to countless people in the whole process mostly drivers, conductors and strangers in the crowds. I was amazed that everyone I interacted with was very polite, cultured and eager to help. I felt rich after this experience.

> "Collect only memories, not things." – Anon

The Closing Bell

"The wise traveler keeps returning to his home."
- African Proverb

In the preface I stated that unlike in a map, the world has no boundaries. Both Deepali and I adjust like a shot wherever we visit. The USA has become like our second home. So was Singapore where both of us lived or England, where I lived in my bachelor days. But still after some length of stay abroad, India calls and we long to return! Why?

We have a doorbell in our apartment in India with a ding dong sound like a church bell. Our eldest grandson on a visit from America during school vacation made an interesting comment, "The number of times the doorbell rings in India each day is several times more than in America."

The statement defines the basic difference in lifestyle in the western world and India. It essentially defines the extent of people to people interaction. Each ringing of the doorbell signifies at least one human contact. The first bell that rings is by the newspaper boy early in the morning, alerting me to pick up the paper outside my door. If I am awake before that, I keep the front door open and say hello to the delivery boy as I pick up the newspaper. This is followed by two more bells soon, one by our domestic help to clean up the house and the other from our cook (Indians love home cooked food). The daily rhythm of human interactions thus starts from the morning.

Subsequent rings of doorbell could be our friends, friends of our grand-children when they are on a visit, a courier boy, or anyone else. It could be from a groceries vendor with his push-cart at the gate of our block, delivering cheese and bread. Or it could be my wife or I returning after getting some groceries from shops within walking distance from our apartment block. Or it could be a friendly neighbor dropping in unannounced! Each ring of the doorbell signifies that human beings are around.

Yes, yes, I start missing the intense human interaction and spontaneous social life in India even at the cost of losing personal space, when I am abroad for too long. One just loves something one is deeply rooted to!

There is something called culture or lifestyle which is distinct in each country, in spite of so many similarities in nature and friendliness of people. In the west, the private space is often a well-protected space of an individual. It is difficult to enter in that space for an outsider or even for a family member. In India relations and friends are natural claimants to the private space. Such differences in culture create a variety without which the world would be very dull.

It is tough to completely cover the amazing variety in this beautiful world of ours. There are a few missing links in my story – Africa, Australia and other exotic places. Often I thought I should make a visit to these places before I close this book. But for quite some time a bell is ringing in my ears - the closing bell. Even the New York stock exchange, the biggest business hub in the world closes every day after a closing bell. But it starts again the next day. I too can sign off for the time being and resume the story another day.

Miles to hop before I stop

ABOUT THE AUTHOR

A renowned technocrat, Utpal Kumar Dutta, enjoys not only his area of specialization in the energy sector, but all aspects of life in general. His interests cover a wide range - from current issues and happenings in the world to music and sports. From reading and savoring a wide range of cuisine to traveling and meeting different people. And all this fuels his desire to write, starting with a book about traveling based on his interactions everywhere, told from his unique upbeat perspective.

www.ingramcontent.com/pod-product-compliance
Lightning Source LLC
Chambersburg PA
CBHW030245030426
42336CB00009B/261